MODERNIZING THE CHINESE DRAGON
The Prospective Impact of Western Aid and Technology on Mainland China

MODERNIZING THE CHINESE DRAGON
The Prospective Impact of Western Aid and Technology on Mainland China

DONALD J. SENESE

Council on American Affairs
1629 K Street N.W., Suite 520
Washington, D.C. 20006

This publication is one of a series of monographs produced by the Council on American Affairs in conjunction with the Council's quarterly *Journal of Social and Political Studies*. Other monographs include *China – The Turning Point; Korea in the World Today; South Africa – The Vital Link; Rhodesia Alone; Sub-Saharan Africa: An Introduction; Sino-Soviet Intervention in Africa; Nicaragua – An Ally Under Siege; The Panama Canal in Perspective; Namibia – The Road to Self-Government; Constitutional Limits to Union Power; Trade Unions and Labor Relations in the U.S.S.R.; American Labor Unions: Political Values and Financial Structure;* and *Saving Social Security.*

Dedicated to Father Raymond de Jaegher who devoted so many years to assist and help the Chinese people in their struggle against tyranny.

Dr. Donald J. Senese, a former college professor and presently a Senior Research Associate, with the House Republican Study Committee, U.S. House of Representatives, has been a longtime student of Asian history and political events.

Dr. Senese received his bachelor's degree in history (1964) from Loyola University in Chicago and his masters (1966) and doctorate (1970) in history from the University of South Carolina in Columbia, South Carolina. Besides graduate study in the field of Asia, he attended Sophia University in Tokyo, Japan, and National Chengchi University in Taipei, Taiwan (Republic of China). As an associate professor of history at Radford College in Radford, Virginia, he taught courses in the History of the Far East (China, Japan, and Korea) and coordinated a number of Asian programs held on campus. He has traveled to the Republic of China on Taiwan, Japan, South Korea, Vietnam, the Phillipines, Macau and Hong Kong.

Besides teaching and traveling, Dr. Senese has written a number of articles on Asian history. His publications include: "Escapes from Mao's 'Paradise': Red China's Terror Unmasked," *Human Events*, December 11, 1971; "Koxinga and A Chinese Restoration: A Defender of the Native Chinese Ming Dynasty Against the Rule of the Manchus," *History Today*, October, 1972; and "Challenge of the Future: The Advancement of the Newly Industrializing Countries," *The Journal of Social and Political Studies*, Fall, 1979. He also contributed chapters to books on Asia: "Korea: Its Role in World History," in *Korea in the World Today* (Washington, D.C.: Council on American Affairs, 1976); "The Historical and Cultural Roots of Modern China" in *China: The Turning Point* (Washington, D.C.: Council on American Affairs, 1976); and "Reassessments for Taiwan, Japan, and South Korea: U.S. Reliability in Asia," in *About Face: The China Decision and Its Consequences* (New Rochelle, New York: Arlington House, 1979).

PREFACE

The United States began 1979 with its recognition of Communist China, abandoning our long-time ally the Republic of China on Taiwan, and began 1980 with extending Most-Favored-Nation (MFN) treatment to the PRC. Despite optimistic forecasts by Carter Administration spokesmen, this shift in policy will have significant ramifications for the United States and the Free World in the years ahead.

While denying MFN to the Soviet Union because of its emigration policies, we extend this principle of nondiscriminatory trade treatment to a regime in Peking seemingly even more brutal and ruthless than that now governing from Moscow. There is no evidence to contradict the fact that the post-Mao Communist leadership is running the same type of regime Mao conducted with its denial of personal, political, economic, cultural, and religious freedom, with its disrespect for human rights, and with its intention to continue a policy of expansionism throughout the world. Just as the promise of the ratification of SALT II did not prevent the Soviets from invading Afghanistan, the promise of recognition, trade, and aid did not prevent the People's Republic of China from invading Vietnam to enforce its will by military force. China and the Soviet Union represent similar strains of Communism.

The granting of MFN to China represents another misstep along a disastrous foreign policy road as we refuse to recognize the clear lessons of aggressors throughout history and seek to appease every new militant totalitarian power. Once these powers gain what they desire from the West, they tend to drop their words of peace and resume their aggressive stance. We built the Soviet Union into a powerful adversary for the Free World through Western technology and Western financing; we appear to be following the same mistaken course regarding Communist China.

Even if there was a strong case which could be made for building up the People's Republic of China as a counterweight to the Soviet Union, our present policymakers are acting in haste without any long-range strategic plan as to where we hope to be in our relations with China in five or ten or fifteen years. Even those who say we need to supply and build up China's technology in oil production as a counter to the Soviet's oil and the possible loss of our present Middle Eastern sources provide us with no guarantee that the U.S. would benefit from China's oil reserves once we help develop them. The U.S. is once again embarking on a policy without a focus, entering a dark tunnel without considering what may be the consequences of entering that tunnel.

Dr. Donald J. Senese has provided a thorough scholarly analysis of the major issues involved in providing technological aid and assistance to Communist China. We cannot ignore the historical lessons of providing such aid to the Soviet Union; we need to consider the consequences of such aid to the Soviet Union; we need to consider the consequences of such a decision regarding China before we go too far along such a tortuous path.

Alexander Solzehnitsyn has warned us of the nature of Communism and the error of trusting the Communists – but the West continues to ignore his warnings to our detriment. By building up one totalitarian power to counter another totalitarian power, we only help create two strong adversaries for the free nations of the world. If we follow the same mistaken policies toward China as we did toward the Soviet Union, we will only be helping to dig deeper the grave for freedom for the West. Read this book carefully. We need to heed the warning in it, and to proceed cautiously before we build up another Communist nation into a world power.

Richard T. Schulze, M.C.

(Representative Richard T. Schulze, first elected to Congress in 1974 to represent Pennsylvania's Fifth Congressional District, is a member of the Subcommittee on Trade of the House Ways and Means Committee.)

Introduction

The People's Republic of China (Communist China) and the United States formally established diplomatic relations January 1, 1979. The U.S., after following a policy of recognizing the Republic of China on Taiwan as the legitimate representative of the Chinese people, joined other Western European nations (Great Britain in 1950, France in 1964, West Germany in 1972) in recognizing the government in Peking as the government of China. The U.S. notified the Republic of China on Taiwan that it planned to terminate its Mutual Defense Treaty of 1954 effective January 1, 1980 but expressed the intention to continue economic relations with Taiwan and to provide a certain level of military support. Relations between the two nations continue through two unofficial but government supported and financed organizations – the United States' American Institute in Taiwan and Taiwan's Coordinating Council for North American Affairs.

The Chinese leadership in Mainland China on October 1, 1979 celebrated thirty years in power. The years of power had been tumultuous ones as the Chinese people underwent a great number of disruptive changes. Consolidation of the rule on the mainland, unsuccessful attempts to incorporate the ROC on Taiwan (e.g., battles over the islands Quemoy and Matsu), major campaigns such as the Hundred Flowers movement to bring out "criticism" of the regime and the "Great Leap Forward," designed to make China an industrial power overnight, characterized the Communist rule in the 1950's. The 1960's witnessed the split between China and its great ally the Soviet Union (leading to bitter denunciations on both sides, rivalry in the Third World, and Sino-Soviet border clashes), the purge of the person once strongly considered Mao Tse-tung's likely successor Liu Shao-chi, and the disruption caused by the Great Proletarian Cultural Revolution. The early 1970's brought new ideological drives and the announcement of the death of another likely Mao successor, Lin Piao, who had been reported killed in a plane crash trying to flee to the USSR after attempting a coup against Mao.

The mid-1970's became a major turning point in Chinese history and brought the struggle for succession to a head in the People's Republic of China. Chou En-Lai, who served as premier, vice-chairman and member of the Politburo Standing

Committee and who had been a close associate of Mao since the Long March of 1935, died on January 8, 1976. Marshal Chu Teh, another longtime associate of Chou and Mao, died in July of 1976. Mao Tse-tung, one of the early founders of the Chinese Communist Party in the 1920's, a dominating spirit for over fifty years for Chinese Communists, the senior living Communist leader and the ruler of China since 1949, died September 9, 1976. Mao's widow, Chiang Ching (who married Mao in 1940) and her followers had been planning to take over in China but a coup displaced her group. This "gang of four," including Mao's widow Chiang Ching, Yao Wen-yuan, Chang Chun-chiao, and Wang Hung-wen, were defeated, arrested in October of 1976, had a campaign of vilification launched against them, and had their supporters purged from the government.

With the passing from the scene of the Communist "seniors" in China, a new group emerged into the leadership. Hua Kuo-feng emerged out of the leadership struggle to become Premier as well as Communist Party leader of China. Teng Hsiao-ping, a close ally of Chou En-lai and Chou's modernization ideas, emerged from previous purges to become Vice-Chairman. A move began to shift China from the chaos of the Cultural Revolution to a period of economic modernization. Consistent with this policy, a number of domestic reforms and changes were initiated (e.g., praise for certain capitalist features in an economy, an admonition to absorb anything "good" from foreign countries) while in the area of foreign policy China reached out to the United States, Japan, and the Western European nations for assistance in advancing in science and developing new technology. The objective would be a modern China by the end of the twentieth century. Part of China's "reassessment" was seeking aid from the West toward modernization and opposing Soviet expansion worldwide.

What type of China will the world face if modernization is achieved? This book will attempt to examine the People's Republic of China's economic structure, some of its past difficulties, and the realistic prospects for its economic future. The role of the United States, which normalized its relations, signed a trade agreement, and has participated in various exchanges (e.g. agricultural missions, education missions), will be examined since China is looking to the United States for substantial assistance in modernization. It will also examine a parallel situation: technological aid by the U.S. and Western European nations to the USSR in an earlier period. Finally, it will look at the possible future benefits of such a policy for the "China Market," long-range international policy effects, and an overall assessment as China moves toward the end of this century. The key question remains: will such scientific and technological assistance aid China to become a responsible and peace-loving member of the world community or will it strengthen China's ability to create mischief and disorder on the world scene?

A note should be taken of transcribing Chinese names into English. The common form has been the Wade-Giles system and one still used by the Chinese in the Republic of China on Taiwan and Hong Kong among others. Effective January 1, 1979, the People's Republic of China, seeking to establish a standardized pronunciation, announced it would use a system called Pinyin (See John E. Cooney, "In Beijing, Xiamen And All Zhongguo, Pinyin is de Rigueur," *The Wall Street Journal*, February 15, 1979, pp. 1 and 22). In order to avoid too much confusion, I have decided to use the Wade-Giles system throughout except for some recent publications which Pinyin is directly used. (Depending on the source, "Peiping" is used in some quotes from the Republic of China publications for "Peking"). A sample of the changes in spelling with the two systems can be seen in this comparison:

Wade-Giles	Pinyin
Amoy	Xiamen
Canton	Guangzhou
Peking	Beijing
Szechuan	Sichuan
Tibet	Xizang
Teng Hsiao-ping	Deng Xiaoping
Mao Tse-tung	Mao Zedong
Chou En-lai	Zhou Enlai
Hsin Hua	Xinhua
China	Zhongguo (not being used)

Early Economic Problems of Communist China

When Mao Tse-tung led his forces to Peking to proclaim the establishment of the People's Republic of China on October 1, 1949, China's economy was in serious disarray resulting from almost three decades of warfare including the war between China and Japan and the civil war between the Communists and the Kuomintang. One of Mao's early tasks would be to reconstruct a viable economic system for China. After consolidating military control and uniting the country under the new Communist leadership, the task of economic reconstruction went forward.

The Chinese Communists needed to adopt an economic recovery program which would bring production up to pre-World War II levels. Two immediate problems concerned re-establishing means of communication throughout the country and controlling rapid inflation. China scholars Franz H. Michael and George E. Taylor in surveying the early years of Communist control noted:

> After an early period of moderation which was necessary in order to minimize the disruption caused by the change-over, they began their brutal program of economic, social, political, and ideological revolution. By the beginning of 1953 the Communists were ready to start on long-range economic planning and to set up a new political structure. (1)

The new leadership in Peking embarked on its first Five Year Plan (1953-1957) which was not designed to raise the living standards of the Chinese people but to create a strong base for industrialization and military power. As for allocation of resources seven times more capital was invested in industry over agriculture with nine-tenths of the industrial allotments going to heavy industry (e.g., steel and iron, electric power). The Chinese were aided by their Russian Communist ally who provided tools, machinery, financial assistance, and technicians. (2)

As a result of intensified activity, industrial production grew, old plants were renovated and expanded while new plants were built, with an expanded railroad system. As part of its program of socialism, eighty per cent of private commercial and industrial firms became state or joint-state enterprises, with nine-tenths of all industrial assets becoming the property of the state. (3) One of the Communist drives or campaigns, entitled the "Five

Anti-Movement" (October 1951-June 1952), was launched against the social class of businessmen in the cities and its eventual result was the elimination of private enterprise in China. (4)

Shortly after he took control of China, Mao Tse-tung and a delegation of high-ranking Chinese Communists went to Moscow (December 16, 1949) and stayed several months talking with Josef Stalin and other Soviet leaders. During this visit, the Treaty of Friendship, Alliance and Mutual Assistance was signed. Important economic developments occurred with the Soviet promise of three hundred million (U.S. dollars) at one per cent interest, provisions for setting up joint Sino-Soviet companies for prospecting, producing, and refining petroleum, coal, gas, and nonferrous metals in Sinkiang were adopted, and important trade and barter agreements came into being. (5)

Following Stalin's death in 1953, Soviet Russia promised additional assistance to China beyond the three hundred million (U.S. dollars) agreed to in the Sino-Soviet Pact in 1950. On September 15, 1953, Li Fu-ch'un, Vice Chairman of the Committee on Finance and Economics, reported back from negotiators in Moscow that the USSR agreed to give China economic and technical assistance in the renovation and construction of one hundred forty one projects of enormous scale by 1959; this promise included fifty projects being built or renovated and ninety-one new projects. Most of the trade would be on a barter basis between the two countries. (6)

The Chinese Communist leadership looked to its ally, the Soviet Union, as the model for technological, industrial, and military advancement. While thousands of Chinese had studied Communism and its operations (e.g., mass organization, political guerrilla warfare) in the Soviet Union beginning in 1921, the Chinese tried to fix the Soviet model (including the Five Year Plan) onto their own country especially attempting to industrialize China as rapidly as possible based on the Soviet model. Technological aid became of tremendous importance. Russian technicians and advisors came as part of the package. Additional technical aid was forthcoming. Despite this aid from the USSR, China had to provide the capital investment for industrialization from its economy. (The capital for this industrialization came from the agricultural production as the Chinese used more and more coercion to get its agricultural workers to produce more. (7) Collectivization of agriculture was especially intensified after July of 1955.) (8)

Problems did occur in China in early 1953. The Chinese subsequently reduced the goals of their first Five Year Plan twice. One of the major goals of the first year became the mobilizing and organizing of the people to make further sacrifices. The Chinese Communists counted heavily on the Soviets to make their industrial construction rapid but problems in the Soviet economy adversely affected the situation in China and China had to reduce its goals. (9)

During early 1956, the socialization of Chinese industry advanced. Beginning in January of 1956, enterprises were nationalized and this in turn was designed to speed up industrialization. A close link continued with the Soviets as they contributed machinery, plants, blueprints, and technical experts to China's program. A linkage was also established by each side of their Central Asian border through extensive railroad development. Mao's reliance and dependence on the Soviet Union had been emphasized in his "lean-to-one-side" slogan. (10)

Certain developments were occurring which would create division between the two giant Communist powers. Khrushchev's attack on Stalin and the "personality cult" at the Twentieth Congress of the Soviet Party brought serious strains between the leaders of both nations. While the Soviets downgraded Stalin, Mao and his followers continued to revere Stalin as a great Marxist-Leninist. Soviet aid was reduced to China supposedly because of problems in Eastern Europe (e.g., 1956 Hungarian Revolution) and Khrushchev began a policy of "peaceful coexistence" with the Western nations without consulting the Chinese Communist leadership. Mao pursued his own policies – the Hundred Flowers campaign, the Great Leap Forward, and the introduction of the communes. Mao became glorified from 1954 onward, similar to the personality cult of Stalin. The early sixties brought ideological battles into the open and Soviet aid for China's economic development came to a halt (e.g., the huge generating plant at the Sanmen gorge on the Yangtze River and the work on the Sinkiang Railroad were two of the projects which came to a standstill). The rivalry intensified between the Chinese Communists and the Soviet Communists for leadership of the world Communist movement; the Chinese labeled the Soviets "modern revisionists" and the Soviets labeled the Chinese as "dogmatists" as each sought its own interpretation of Marxism-Leninism for the contemporary world. (11) China's great support for technological aid ended as the Chinese-Soviet split became more pronounced. As far as the Soviets were concerned, the Sino-Soviet split put China completely on its own resources for industrial development.

China's Post-Mao Modernization Program

The Chinese Communist leadership under Hua Kuo-feng and Teng Hsiao-ping has based its program to make China modern and industrialized on a campaign called the "four modernizations" focusing on development of agriculture, industry, defense, and technology. The strategy of the four modernizations urges action to readjust, reform, correct, and improve." One observer has noted that the dreams as envisioned by posters seek to develop a future for China which is a cross "between that of H.G. Wells and the science fiction of *Star Wars*." (12)

The major role of technology is an important ingredient in the unfolding of China's future. The Communist Party line calls on workers to actively develop science, train personnel, and speed the introduction of technology and exports. Stress has been placed on boosting production as well as gaining control over the increases in population. Seeking lessons from the field of economics, workers are exhorted to study the rules of economic management so they can strengthen price management and guarantee price stability by readjusting any price which is unreasonable. (13)

China's openness to new ideas became apparent with various statements of the post-Mao era leaders. Some observers traced the origin of major economic and military modernization back to 1964 when the idea was promoted by the late Premier Chou En-lai. Chairman Hua Kuo-feng had outlined his modernization program during 1978 and was supposed to have ordered its acceleration. During the 1978 National Day ceremonies celebrating the Communist victory on October 1, 1949, the theme stressed included a push for speedy modernization even including borrowing good things from foreign countries. During the middle of the month of October, the head of the Academy of Social Sciences, Hu Chiao-mu, a veteran theorist, asserted that methods in capitalist countries should be studied since they had experience and had become proficient at applying economic laws. Thus, he added, the Chinese proletariat could learn from the bourgeoise. Turning back to the period of the Great Leap Forward in 1958, Hu observed that since that time wages and productivity did not increase and China's industrial growth came solely from a larger workforce. Hu used a lengthy article in the *People's Daily* to stress the need for continued socialist planning, to outline some new guidelines for economic reorganization and to recognize the superiority of capitalism in some spheres (e.g., agriculture production and management in the United States). (14)

The early ambitious program of a rapid modernization in the next few years for China (e.g., targets of sixty million tons of steel and four hundred million tons of grain by 1985) was somewhat scaled down during the second plenum of the Fifth National People's Congress (held in late June and early July, 1979). The overall thrust of Premier Hua Kuo-feng's new three year program to "readjust, restructure, consolidate and improve" the national economy was to welcome direct foreign investment and the acceptance of loans from foreign banks, a marked change from its previous thirty years of economic practice, Additional changes became evident as special export-oriented zones were developed (e.g., near the city of Shanghai) and the granting of commercial authority to some provinces to deal directly with foreign firms (e.g. Kwangtung and Fukien). Despite this obvious readjustment, Communist China's goal remained economic modernization. (15)

China's major thrust in the three year program allocates greater emphasis on agriculture and light industry but heavy industry still receives a heavy concentration of resources. The respective split in emphasis has been:

	1978	1979
Heavy Industry	54.7%	46.8%
Light Industry	5.4%	5.8%
Agriculture	10.7%	14.7%

Agriculture, light industry (especially textiles) and five high priority industrial sectors (coal, oil, power generation, building materials, and transportation and communications) will receive favorable treatment in imports over the next few years. (16)

China has sought to attract additional attention by such

measures as its Chinese-foreign joint equity venture law (unveiled on July 1, 1979) designed to encourage foreign investment. The director of the foreign trade department of the Peking Foreign Trade Institute, Professor Liu Chao-jin, stated that China would seek cooperation with foreign companies in a variety of areas: electric power industry (e.g., hydro, thermal, and nuclear); energy resources (e.g., oil and coal); transport and communication (e.g., plastics and construction materials); precision machinery; electronics; iron, steel and nonferrous minerals; agricultural mechanization. These joint ventures, he observed, would primarily produce items for export and may be used in the domestic market if such items can replace what China may need to import. Chen Jie, Vice Minister for Foreign Trade, revealed that despite the readjustment both imports and exports would continue to grow. (17)

The recent activities of the Chinese Communists in opening a door to the West for advanced technology have to be seen in perspective. It is only by a thorough analysis of the Chinese economy and its economic policies that the observer can realize the significance of the Soviet withdrawal, the internal disruption in China which delayed its advancement and resulted in the backward state of China's economy, and the need to make the necessary contacts to secure the technology of the Western nations.

The Chinese economy had been ravaged by the Great Cultural Revolution. Hua Kuo-feng had charged that the activities of the "gang of four" between 1974 to 1976 had brought the entire Chinese economy close to collapse drastically affecting total industrial output and losing about twenty-eight million tons just in steel production alone. (18) The Chinese Communists have openly recognized and admitted many of the weaknesses in their own economy.

One of the concerns of the leaders of the People's Republic of China centers on the need for scientific achievements in carrying out its modernization goals. In its poster campaigns China has stressed that "the level of science of the entire nation be greatly raised" as part of its efforts stressing that advances in science and technology are necessary if China is to catch up with advanced countries by the end of the century. During a conference of six thousand scientific experts, China adopted a scientific development plan for 1985 with emphasis in the eight areas of agriculture, energy materials, electronic computers, lasers, space science and technology, high-energy physics, and genetic engineering. The program is a significant part of China's "four modernizations." China is counting heavily on the United States' scientific and technical capabilities to help meet these goals. (19)

Some of the leading Chinese economists criticized the tendency in the 1970's to develop heavy industry in isolation from and at the expense of agriculture and light industry. It was noted that over a lengthy period:

> an economic structure had gradually been formed which took steel as the key and had everything arranged to serve steel production. This was in turn geared to heavy industrial needs, and expansion of the sectors providing for consumer needs was neglected. Under these circumstances, although heavy industry expanded and national output value increased, the life of the people improved very little. (20)

One Chinese publication compared the present state of China to a giant ship sailing the sea which had been damaged and diverted from its course by Lin Piao and the "gang of four." The task was to repair the ship and bring it back to its true course. Collectivism was advocated. Opposition was urged to both anarchism and bureaucracy. Nothing, it urged, should interfere with the goal of achieving the "four modernizations."(21)

A meeting of over one hundred of Shanghai's economists (including members of the Shanghai Academy of Social Sciences, the Shanghai Municipal Economic Society, and the editorial department of the *Academic Monthly*), met to discuss socialist production. The stress was on improving "the people's standard of living," an objective which was lost because of the "interference and sabotage" of Lin Piao and the "gang of four." The answer to the proportionate relation between accumulation and consumption, between production and livelihood, and the various economic sectors had to be answered in accord with "Marxism-Leninism-Mao Zedong Thought." (22)

China looks to the United States, its "former" adversary, as playing a major part in its plans for modernization. The Chinese press publicized the first annual meeting of one hundred eighty Chinese economists, professors, and research fellows from throughout the country who met in Chengdu "to discuss and exchange views on recent developments in the U.S. economy." The sponsoring group was the U.S. Economics Association, a Chinese academic society established the previous October. While the conference discussed China-U.S. trade relations and the future prospects, there was emphasis "on seeking ways and means to apply U.S. advanced technology and experiences to speed up China's modernization program."(23) Yet, a crucial question remains over what China will use this technology for in future years as well as what future policies, especially toward the United States, China will adopt. Can the United States expect future good relations with China and an expanding U.S.-China trade as part of its benevolence in aiding the modernization of China's science and technology? It is a question which some answer must be provided before the United States embarks on a major foreign policy and economic assistance program directed toward the People's Republic of China.

Technological Aid to the Soviets: A Case Study for China?

There are numerous means of transferring technology: importation of complete plants; importation of new machinery for capital investment and for copying; international movement of scientists, engineers, and technicians (e.g. construction and start up of plants, students studying overseas); and importation of printed matter (e.g., books, scientific reports and periodicals) providing a constant stream of new knowledge. Economists do recognize that modern economic growth is increasingly dependent on technological change. (24)

As China begins to open its doors to expanded trade and development, the nations of the Western world, particularly the United States, will have to face the question of providing technology to China and on what level. Besides trade in nonstrategic goods, how much should be provided China in the field of advanced industrial technology, particularly technology which might have a military purpose? And, a major question will depend on how China intends to use this technology. The Western nations have an example they can look at in history and examine – technology and aid provided to the former ally of China, the Soviet Union. An examination of this experience should help to give some insight into the ramifications of aiding China in a similar way.

The Communists triumphed in 1917 in Russia, a nation

which was experiencing serious economic problems especially from its involvement in World War I. The United States began its policy of active trading with the Communist regime in Russia in 1918, even before the Communists' entire control had been established over the whole country. This action took place during the presidential term of Woodrow Wilson, and the theory was expounded that rather than attempt a policy of blockade and economic isolation of Bolshevik-occupied Russia, it would be better for the United States to begin a policy of trading in the hopes that improved economic conditions for the Russian people would assist in the establishment of a stable and proper government in Russia and would help bring about a moderate and stable social order. (25)

Lenin sought to build the Soviet nation through centralized control which was as productive as the most advanced Western nation and viewed Western aid and assistance as vital to this task. Lenin's view of Russian history attributed the prerevolutionary industrial growth of Russia as one based on exploitation of the workers by the capitalist class and thus had brought backwardness to the Russian worker. When Lenin presented his New Economic Policy, effective in 1921, he viewed concessions to Western entrepreneurs as part of the central mechanism of technology transfer. It would include technical assistance contracts, employment of foreign engineers and experts in the USSR, and having Soviet experts trained in the West. During this period of the middle 1920's, over two hundred concessions were made to foreign firms. The Soviets did not attempt to develop new mechanisms for domestic productions. Attempts to experiment with new mechanisms were limited and shortlived, and then abandoned. Concentration was on acquiring new productive processes from the West, establishing research institutes, and training engineers. Much of the rapid growth of the 1920's depended on foreign operations and technical skills. (26)

The Soviets gained great economic benefits from Western nations by pure concession or the joint venture for the transfer of Western skills and technology. After 1928, the Soviets moved to rely more on technical assistance agreements and individual work contracts with foreign companies, engineers, skilled workers and consultants. The Soviets eliminated the previous policy of concessions and joint ventures through such devices as breach of contract, taxation, and physical force. The new system after 1928 denied capitalist firms any share of ownership and placed the entire control of technology transfer operations into the hands of the Soviet government. While the Soviets concluded many wide-ranging technical assistance agreements with foreign firms in 1929, they included some of the largest projects in the world and the contracts were under specific, limited duration. There was a large influx of foreign technology in the form of skilled labor as well as technical data and equipment. Even after these experts left (most were gone by 1932) there were left behind the designs based on Western models. These designs made a major contribution to the great increases in manufacturing capacity of the Soviet Union. Experts have recognized that until 1941 the production increases in most Soviet industrial sectors resulted from the installation and expansion of Western plants acquired in the massive transfer of technology which took place in the brief period only a few years earlier. (27)

W. Averell Harriman, former U.S. Ambassador to Russia, reported to the State Department in June, 1944 that the Soviet leader Josef Stalin paid tribute to the assistance provided by the United States to Soviet industry before and after World War II and Stalin had estimated that about two thirds of all the large industrial enterprises in the Soviet Union had been built with United States help or technical assistance. Assistance to the remaining third had been provided by other Western nations such as Germany, France, Britain, Sweden and Italy. The Soviets had given the military a priority in industrialization and used the technology to develop its military machine. (28)

Evidence indicates clearly that the USSR is reliant on Western aid via low-interest, long-term credits and advanced technology while it continues to build its military machinery. Thus Western technology aids the industrial sector of the USSR economy, releases scarce resources for the military sector, and aids the Soviets in closing the technological gap in the strategic force domain. (29)

Surveying Western economic aid to the Soviet Union and the continued growth of the Soviet military machinery, Alexander Wolynski focused on the major role the United States played in this development:

The pivot of economic co-operation with the West had to

be the United States, the most technologically advanced country, which has the industrial and financial potential needed for the realization of the Kremlin's big projects. Moreover, owing to some geographical similarities, the Americans had the expertise for dealing with problems arising from the space and climatic conditions of the Soviet Union. It could also be expected that the American example would encourage other Western countries to embark on big-scale economic co-operation with Moscow. (30)

One of the basic issues from the first dealings with Russia under Communist leadership was how to protect national security and advance international political policy without limiting the international earning power of the United States. Export controls by the United States, first instituted in 1940 to assure the availability of scarce materials and strengthen national defense, emerged as a mechanism to review the transfer of certain technology to Communist nations when the argument was made that the transfer of technology to Communist countries imperils the national security of the United States. It has sometimes been difficult to ascertain which particular technologies or products will or will not strengthen the capabilities of potentially hostile nations. (31)

The United States Congress acted to use export controls as part of a national security policy by exacting the first comprehensive authority for export restrictions ever legislated by Congress in peace time with the adoption of the Expert Control Act of 1949. The measure aimed to deny the Soviet Union any trade which contributed either to its military or economic potential. It was clear that to be effective the United States needed to secure the cooperation of other Western nations to implement it. A Coordinating Committee (COCOM) of the Consultative Group (formed in 1949 to implement the controls) put together a roster of controls to ban the sale of goods of strategic military values to all Communist powers. The United States enacted the Mutual Defense Assistance Control Act of 1951 (or Battle Act) which required an embargo on the shipment of arms, ammunitions and other strategic projects and materials to any nation or nations which threatened the security of the United States (including the Soviet Union and countries under its domination) and required a cut off of military, economic, and financial aid to any country refusing to cooperate with U.S. sponsored trade controls. (COCOM was not successful because the U.S. allies in Western Europe and Japan sought out trade with the USSR separating the political issues and trade operations.) The U.S. liberalized its restrictions on the export of goods and technology to the Soviet Union with the adoption of the Export Administration Act of 1969, but did prohibit exports that would make a significant contribution to the military potential of the Soviet Union while lifting the ban on those products and technologies that would merely strengthen the USSR's economic potential. During this period of detente, arguments were made that this new policy would help correct the U.S. trade deficit, open new trade markets, provide more overseas opportunities to U.S. businessmen, and improve cooperation and political relations between the US and USSR. A move toward a stricter national security consideration came with the Export Administration Act Amendments of 1977, allowing the Defense Department to review exports to any country (not just Communist nations) and to develop better criteria for determining what exports (e.g. technologies, commodities) should be controlled. (32)

The major criticism of the Export Administration Acts of 1969 and 1977 centered on the premise that controls on items of military potential were not enough for U.S. national security. It was argued that the Soviets were seeking U.S. technological know-how which had important military implications under supposed commercial agreements. It is impossible at times to adequately separate the link between civilian and military production technologies. (33)

U.S. Congressman Robert K. Dornan of California, one critic of the export of technology to the Soviet Union especially technology which can be used for military purposes, has pointed out the difficulties of ascertaining the significance of some exchanges:

> It is all too easy to overlook a seemingly minor or peripheral issue, only to find later that it has ingeniously been converted into a conduit for the Soviet acquisition of a major U.S. technology. (34)

Thus, one of the complications has been the category of goods known as "dual technologies" which can be used for both civil and military purposes. These items include integrated circuits which can be used for missile guidance systems as well as the civilian uses in products like pocket calculators, digital wrist watches and television sets. In addition, there are computers which can be used for more sophisticated weapons systems and civilian uses like keeping track of business records, communications, etc. While export of forty-five of the Centalign-B ball bearing grinding machines had been stopped in 1961, the U.S. in 1972 allowed the Soviets to acquire one hundred sixty four of these Centalign-B precision grinding machines; the Soviets have used these machines to produce ball bearings to produce MIRV warheads and it has aided MIRV technology for the Soviets. (35)

The AFL-CIO Executive Council in the United States expressed concern that the transfer of technology weakens U.S. superiority in various technological fields and contributes to the buildup of the Soviet military machine:

> Many of these technologies have direct military application for such weapons as independent multiple warheads, armor piercing rockets, and submarine detection devices. Others help indirectly to build military capability by increasing industrial efficiency, thereby allowing greater diversion of resources from the consumer to the military sector. Still others are useful to the secret police for repressing the courageous activities of the Soviet dissidents. (36)

The great deficiency of the Soviets has been not in scientific knowledge but in production knowledge. Thus the Soviets seek to buy not the plans but the knowledge that would allow them to build their own production facilities. They can construct these facilities with all the systems and quality control which U.S. defense plants possess. (37)

The Soviets have sought to maximize military power while importing technological innovation from the Western world. While the Soviets may never catch up to the Western nations in economic terms, their program of substitution of certain resources will allow them to stay close enough to the Western industrial powers in science and technology while they can continue to achieve pre-eminence in those sectors which they see militarily important. (38)

The Soviets thus continue to stockpile, harden and dispense their industrial and economic assets and give no evidence that they are reducing defense research and development or industrial capacity to divert them to other areas. On the contrary, estimates for 1975 had to be revised showing that the Soviets are devoting eleven to thriteen percent of their GNP, rather than five to seven percent, to defense spending and that a basic Soviet strategy remains the achievement of superiority in deployed military technology by the early 1980's. The Soviets have operated to use detente as part of their strategy for global dominance. (39)

Alexander Wolynski has pointed out that large credits extended to Soviet Russia and other Warsaw Pact countries have made possible important transfers of technology, all of which have direct military significance. (40)

Soviet domestic policy historically has been unable to create new technologies which could significantly expand Soviet military potential and industrial productivity and has relied on Western technology to remedy its inefficiencies. Such assistance not only makes up for Soviet shortcomings but also increases the military-industrial potential of the USSR.(41)

The Soviets have made extensive use of Western technology in many different ways while carrying on a foreign policy hostile to the goals of the United States and the Free World. While the United States had established itself as the leading developer of computer technology by the early 1950's, the Soviet Union's development and upgrading of its computer technology has been clearly "dependent on a substantial and sustained transfer of technology from the West, particularly the United States." (42)

The approval of export licensing for the sale of oil drilling technology to the Soviet Union, particularly the export of a $144 million oil drill bit factory by Dresser Industries which will produce 100,000 drill bits each year, raised serious questions over the wisdom of such a sale. The Dresser plant will allow them to divert more resources for use in the military sector while the sale included two items which have important military potential: the tungsten carbide used in the oil drill bits can be used to produce armor piercing projectiles and the computerized electronic beam welding machine can assist in manufacturing jet aircraft and can be used for nuclear and laser applications. Soviet production will be high producing about one third of the 300,000 drill bits the U.S. produces as the world's leading producer of drill bits. These bits will exceed Soviet capacity. The United States has helped subsidize a potential competitor for the production and sale of high technology oil drilling equipment. (43) Antony Sutton has documented the wide range of Soviet military equipment which has resulted from Western aid: Soviet missiles with American accelerometers; small instruments used to measure gravitational pull; American ball bearings; American built plants for Soviet tanks and armored cars; Soviet tank designs based on American and British designs. (44)

One of the most recent and controversial technological exchanges involved the building of the largest truck factory in the world, a plant situated on the Kama River with a potential annual output of 100,000 multi-axle ten ton trucks, trailers, and off-the road vehicles. Key design, engineering and equipment came from the U.S. It has been recognized by more and more individuals of the great military potential of the Kama plant. CIA official Hans Heymann and Lawrence J. Brady, then acting director of the Office of Export Administration, testified before a Congressional committee in May 1979 that diesel engines from the Kama plant had been diverted to military use and that vehicles containing these engines were used in military formations of the Warsaw Pact. The Kama plant-produced engines also are going into armored personnel carriers and assault vehicles. (The U.S. Department of Commerce has officially denied these reports.) Yet the export licenses granted, especially one filed December 12, 1971, specifically stated that the Kama plant would manufacture trucks for civilian use. Specific military use is being made of a major plant facility built with Western technology and aid. (45)

Despite the concern over the technology question, how significant has trade been with the Soviet Union and the Warsaw Bloc nations? As the Communist nations seek new Western goods, it has expanded. Trade volume with the Soviets has jumped from $191 million in 1970 to $2.8 billion in 1978 while trade with the Communist bloc overall has gone from $579 million to more than $6 billion during this same period. (46) Yet, the $2.8 billion trade with the Soviets, a record high, has been achieved after many false starts over sixty years; this $2.8 billion still represents just over one-third the amount of trade carried on with the Republic of China on Taiwan in 1979. Yet, the great lure for businessmen has been the potential market, not yet realized, of trade with the USSR even though historical precedent does little to justify such optimism. (47)

Technology – its use and denial – is a powerful tool in the hands of the United States and the Free World. In the case of the Soviets, it seems that there has been little beneficial results to Western nations but great benefit to the Soviets. After a study of trade between the Soviets and the U.S., Carl Gershman issued this warning:

> It is difficult to speculate on future trends inside the Soviet Union and more difficult to influence them from outside. If we have learned anything at this late date in our relations with the USSR it is that interaction with the West does not necessarily yield helpful results, and that the rich creations of a free system become distorted when absorbed by a system that is not free. Those who wish to build bridges to the East through trade might recall that Brezhnev, on the eve of detente, observed that "scientific-technical progress has now become one of the main bridgeheads of the historical struggle of the two systems."
>
> It would be ironic if the one system able to generate such progress lost the struggle because it lacked the wisdom to understand its advantage and the will to protect it. (48)

Deficiencies of the PRC in Science and Technology

The task of modernizing science and technology has been targeted as key reforms to achieve the "four modernizations" but the backwardness of China's science and technology has been and will continue to be a major problem. When China underwent the turmoil of the "Great Cultural Revolution," the older generation of trained scientists and technical specialists were denounced and labeled as opponents of the Communist regime (e.g. "rightists," "capital roaders," "reactionary academic authorities," "imperialist spies"). They were part of the large number of individuals who were sent to the countryside to be "reeducated" suffering humiliations, persecutions, and torture. Thus, during the years of the Cultural Revolution, scientific and technical research was in a vacuum. This movement tended to widen what had been a narrowing gap with the advanced world nations in the fields of science and technology. With the overthrow of the "gang of four" (e.g., they were arrested in October, 1976, one month after Mao's death), many of the older generation of scientists and technical experts were brought back, rehabilitated and restored to their former positions and posts of authority. The problem of the gap in scientific and technical knowledge could not be resolved this easily: these older scientists and technicians were advanced in age, some were in a weakened state of health, all were bitter at the treatment they had received, and the time period had dislocated and alienated them from the new achievements in science and technology. These people will be of little benefit or use as China seeks to accelerate its gains in science and technology.

What about the younger generation of potential scientists and technicians? During the early state of the Cultural Revolution, classes at colleges and universities were stopped so students could make revolution. These colleges and universities were closed for four years. While achievement tests had been used to enroll promising students in various academic fields, the Chinese Communists adopted an "education reform" which the candidates for enrollment in the colleges and universities had to meet the tests of being politically and ideologically active as recommended by the worker-farmer masses. As expected, this change caused unqualified students to find their way into the higher educational system, grades of students plummeted, and Chinese education was left in a shambles and in chaos. For example, a number of university graduates in 1977 were assigned to Shanghai for training in science and technology systems. The examinations they had taken were virtually on the middle school level and, even at that reduced level of testing competency, the results were not encouraging for a nation seeking rapid advancement in the fields of science and technology: sixty-eight per cent could not pass the test on mathematics, seventy per cent failed in physics, seventy six per cent flunked chemistry. Some were so ill-prepared that they turned in blank test papers. (49)

• The "four modernizations" had to look to bring in new scientific and technological knowledge from abroad. While the Chinese Communists prepared to dispatch large numbers of students for advanced education overseas, it became difficult to find qualified college and university students and graduates to participate. They were limited to sending out a limited number of students who had been graduated from universities before the Cultural Revolution – a group who are mostly over the age forty-five and are presently professors, associate professors, lecturers, or researchers. Although the Chinese leadership has proclaimed China will need eight hundred thousand scientists and technicians before the year 1985, they presently possess about three hundred thousand to four hundred thousand scientists and technicians of which there are only about sixty thousand qualified scientists and engineers. (50) It is a figure far short of China's projected needs and it seems unlikely that China will be able to train and cultivate that many trained professionals in the short span of seven or eight years.

Evidence is abundant that the technical standards of Chinese Communist workers have much room for improvement and are unsatisfactory for China's needs. The Cultural Revolution acted as a detriment for workers wanting to learn technology since once a worker had mastered a technique, he was likely to be removed or transferred. The newly recruited worker usually did not receive strict technical training and lacked advanced operational skills. The technical level of some of the workers dated back to the period of the 1960's, and in some cases, the 1950's. (51)

According to one survey by the Chinese Communist National Federation of Labor Unions, a review of twenty-six provinces, cities, and autonomous districts, the cultural and technical levels of employees and workers rated low. It was reported that 81.4 per cent of the textile workers were on a cultural level below junior middle schools (of which 8.3 per cent were illiterate or semi-illiterate). The Chinese enforce an eight-grade wage system with grade eight being on top and grade one the lowest. Since seventy per cent of the workers are graded below three, it is obvious that overall technical skills of the workers are on the lower end. It appears that among the leading cadres in the workshops and laboratories, very few have a grasp on modern scientific management. (52)

This low level of technical skills has contributed to low labor productivity of the enterprises, a shoddy quality of products turned out, excessive unusuable materials, and a great amount of wastefulness in production enterprises.

As mentioned earlier, the Chinese, with the aid of the Soviet Union during the period of friendship, established about two hundred modern, large scale factories. The technical standards of these enterprises were high and China was having to bear tremendous cost in capital. These factories would require employment for skilled technical people and did little for China's task of creating expanded job opportunities for a large, unskilled population.

Mao Tse-tung in 1958 put forward a formula of simultaneous advancement of large enterprises along with middle and small enterprises urging a simultaneous implementation of native method production and Western method production. He stressed the industrial construction in order to promote the road of "independence and sovereignty" as well as "self-reliance and rejuvenation." He called for relying on the masses in renovating technology, and opposed bringing in large quantities of advanced technology and equipment from abroad. In fact, Mao attacked those relying on foreign country technology and equipment as being possessed of a "foreign slave philosophy" and "compradore's idea." The Cultural Revolution heightened this opposition to foreign technology and the program to introduce advanced technology and equipment from foreign countries had been completely suspended.

The Chinese Communists have a major problem with their production equipment which is far behind modern standards. Overall the large and middle enterprises of the Chinese Communists can be divided into three categories: 1) enterprises in existence when the Communists gained control of the mainland in 1949; 2) enterprises built by the Soviet Union and Eastern Bloc countries in the 1950's; and 3) enterprises from Western Europe, Japan, and other Free World countries in the early 1960's. An examination of each category of these enterprises presents an understanding of China's present economic plant equipment.

When the Communists gained control of the Chinese mainland in 1949, their takeover of twenty eight hundred enterprises left behind by the government of Chiang Kai-shek became the basis for the Chinese Communist "state-operated enterprises." They added to this all privately operated enterprises which became public-private joint operated enterprises during the early period of socialist reform. Further, the Chinese Communists built other "state-operated enterprises" and "local state-operated enterprises" over the past thirty years as part of their spirit of self-reliance. Although the category of these enterprises may be very large, the majority of their facilities which were built in the 1940's or even earlier are outdated, and their production efficiency is poor.

During the period of China-USSR friendship, a total of two hundred seventy enterprises were built in the 1950's, with Soviet assistance contributing to about two hundred and those built with Eastern European (Communist Bloc) assistance numbering about sixty eight. These enterprises brought new branches of industry to China – manufacturing of automobiles, tractors, aircraft, precision instruments, heavy mining metallurgical equipment, machine tools, ball bearings, giant powered machinery, electronics and chemical industries. These enterprises enabled the Chinese Communists to lay down the initial foundation of industrialization and constituted the backbone of Chinese Communist industry. (53) Yet, a good part of the Soviet machinery and equipment was coarse and cumbersome, lacking adequate precision and being poor in efficiency. Such production machinery dating back to the 1950's or before and needs modernization and replacement.

A third category of enterprises was acquired from 1963 to 1966 when relations with the Soviets were on a downturn. Western Europe, Japan, and other Free World nations supplied China with about forty plants with complete equipment. These were set up during the period of the Cultural Revolution. During the latter half of 1972, the Chinese Communists purchased newer model plants from Europe, the United States, and Japan. By the end of 1978, these orders totaled about one hundred thirty plants with some still being erected. The forty plants of the early 1960's and the one hundred thirty of the 1970's constituted plants with the most modern and sophisticated equipment.

After the death of Mao Tse-tung, a push began by the new leadership taking firm control for China to bring in advanced technology and equipment from foreign countries. Citations were made of post-World War II Japan as a case to be imitated. In the period of more than a decade after the 1960's, Japan had brought in over twenty two thousand patents on advanced technology from abroad, collecting the best examples from all over the world. Since this was a crucial factor in Japan's phenomenal economic success, China was being told that it should imitate Japan in following these steps. (54) Calls were increased in official publications for bringing in sophisticated equipment from foreign nations. For example, during 1978, a whole series of contracts were signed for new technology and complete sets of equipment with manufacturers in Western European nations, Japan, and other areas. One estimate from Peking stated that the total value of these contracts exceeded those accumulated from 1972 thru 1976. (55)

As the Chinese leadership had to pull back its ambitious goals in mid-1979 compared to the earlier optimistic 1979 statements, a similar situation developed with these ambitious contracts. China found some of these contracts greatly strained its ability to pay in foreign exchange and thus it was forced to suspend and cancel some of these contracts early in 1979. (56)

Chinese Communist industry overall suffers from dilapidated equipment and outdated technology. As in socialist economies few leaders pay heed to the idea of economic efficiency in running enterprises. While management is substandard, enterprises are plagued with the problems of a lack of steady labor, lack of production quotas, lack of quality control, and lack of cost accounting. (57) Production consumes more raw material and power than necessary. Economic returns from these enterprises have been disappointing because of squandering too much manpower, low productivity, poor quality of items produced, prodigious waste, and high costs.

The post-Mao leadership in China is concerned with past difficulties. Even the National Science Conference, which opened in Peking March 18, 1978, stressed that more emphasis needed to be placed on economic development and that science, technology, and pragmatism would be critical in achieving this goal of the "four modernizations" in agriculture, industry, national defense, science and technology. As part of this development, emphasis may be on giving scientists and technicians more power. It was Hua Kuo-feng who announced the decision to dissolve revolutionary committees and put professional managers at the head of factories, production brigades, schools, colleges, shops, party organizations, government organizations, and other enterprises. (58)

Current policies have put an emphasis on managerial and technical responsibility. Divisions still exist over the specifics of the modernization policy. One observer, after examining the industrial relations field in China, has stated that it is not clear whether China possesses the convertible resources to modernize rapidly across all sectors of the economy in the manner envisioned. (59)

Productivity efficiency remains a major problem for the Chinese Communists. The steel industry production, for example, is still on the level of the 1950's – a Japanese steel worker produces an average of three hundred tons of steel per year whereas the Chinese Communist worker produces about ten tons, a disparity of thirty times. (60) The thermal energy put into smelting three tons of steel in Communist China can be used to produce five tons of steel in the industrialized countries. (61) Synthetic ammonia-producing chemical fertilizer plants consume forty times more of electricity than in the more advanced industrial nations. (62) The Chinese Communists have admitted publicly that they have a twenty-eight per cent effective use of fuel – almost one half of the fifty per cent effective use in industrially developed nations. (63)

Aside from inefficiencies in the use of production tools, China's industrial products have been of poor quality, e.g. cotton cloth which shrinks in water and fades in color, television sets which have a limited life span, tractors which have been substandard and in many cases unusable. (64)

China, especially since the Cultural Revolution, has suffered from serious mismanagement in industrial production. This has been combined with poor economic planning and the resulting failure to develop a coordination of proper relations among the various segments of the national economy to insure efficient and steady economic performance. The leading defects in the economy include: serious imbalance between agriculture and industry; a disproportion between light and heavy industries; a lack of coordination between accrual and consumption, especially the tendency to belittle consumption of the people and accentuating accumulation; excessively large capital construction, which has stretched China's financial and material resources too thin; the imbalance between supplies of fuel, electricity, and raw materials with the requirements of industry (e.g., emphasis on steel production while investments for coal, electric power, transportation and construction materials associated with heavy industry have been low); a failure to relate new construction projects with existing production requirements.

The latter problem cited was illustrated by the construction of the steel cutting plant of the Wuhan steel company, which was built with equipment imported from West Germany at a cost of three hundred twenty five million (U.S. dollars). When construction was completed at the end of 1978, it was discovered that there was not electricity in the Wuhan area to power the new plant in full capacity of operation. (65)

The Ching-lin plant, attached to the Shanghai petrochemical factory, had been designed to produce forty seven thousand tons of synthetic wool annually or almost one half of China's annual output of natural wool. Because of a failure to put in additional wool weaving and spinning facilities, the reels of fibre of wool turned out by the plant could find no takers. The situation continued with such a pile up of surplus fibre that eventually production was stopped. A shift was made to producing a cotton-type fibre – but it caused delay, a slowdown in production, added investment in the plant facilities, and raised costs of production. (66)

China's means of developing capital funds are much different from Western nation enterprises, and different from what many entrepreneurs would view as sound economic policy. The Chinese Communist leadership has adopted a policy of low wages and low income for the large masses of workers and farmers. As for the production and marketing of products, the policy is low cost to produce and a high selling price for a healthy profit for the state operated enterprises. The money made by these state enterprises and handed over to the state constitute well over ninety per cent of Chinese Communist revenues. (67) There is no private investment in China's socialist economy. And the proposed plan to develop China's national economy through to 1985 calls for funds in the neighborhood of six hundred billion (U.S. dollars). (68) Analyst Shannon R. Brown has noted:

> In view of the power that the government of the PRC has to organize and direct economic activity, the pace of technological change achieved in the past quarter century must be considered modest. The apparent reason for the record is a combination of excessive dependence on the Soviet Union in the 1950's (which created enormous problems when the Soviets withdrew their advisors), the Maoist preoccupation with equity and cultural revolution, and functional deficiencies in some of China's economic

institutions. (69)

Examining China's financial operations, it appears this is an unrealistic target based on past and current performances. Teng Hsiao-ping admitted that the capital fund for carrying out this ambitious plan of development is short by at least three hundred billion (U.S. dollars). (70)

Despite any additional flow of funds from Japan and Western nations to assist China's need for advanced technology, a remaining problem is China's central economic management system, a duplicate of the Soviet planned economy in the Stalin era in Soviet Russia. The planning mechanism of the Chinese Communist economy goes from the top (e.g., central leadership control) down to local units. Everything must be approved at the highest level. The mandatory plans are managed excessively and rigidly and serve to suffocate any independent nature of local units. An enterprise is thus responsible only to the superior and to the plan. This system eliminates any flexibility or the ability to cope with new developments or contingencies.

One of the major economic problems has been on pricing. Since the economic plan adopted may not have been worked out meticulously, the pricing of products does not always reflect the capital investment and labor which went into making a specific product. Some products easily manufactured could bring in a high profit while some that have gone through a difficult process could earn little in return. Deficiencies in this system become evident: production value and quantity may be pursued; variety and quality may be ignored; market demands may be overlooked. Production may be geared to turning out easily made goods while there is less production for items which are not technically as easy to make. The end result is a distorted market with items produced of a low value and little profit. Chaos results as unneeded goods are produced, and production and demand are dislocated. One example often cited of this problem is in China's steel production, which even the Chinese leadership admit is sluggish. Chinese industry suffers from a serious shortage of raw steel to produce steel plates, zinc-covered steel plates, and steel tubes which are light in weight but require a complicated production process. Yet, items such as commonplace corner steel and medium size round steel which requires a relatively simple technique to produce are overstocked and pile up a huge inventory. When in 1977, the Chinese planned to produce sixty thousand lathes, the result was an annual production of one hundred ninety nine thousand simple type lathes, more than triple the number called for in the original plan, while the larger, more complicated high precision lathes went unproduced. The 1978 plan called for seventy thousand lathes and one hundred eighty three thousand simple lathes were actually produced. (71)

The Chinese system of financial management appears to bring the most inefficient result possible. An enterprise does not have any capital fund it can readily use.If there is need for putting in additional machinery or equipment or other features, the enterprise submits an application to the chief planner, secures an approval, and then the enterprise can put in the requested equipment without any costs to the enterprise itself. The enterprise then is immune to any economic obligations and has no need to feel concerned about how the equipment will be used especially whether it will be used in an efficient or uneconomic manner and if there will be any means to secure beneficial returns from the investment. If the application for new equipment is turned down, the enterprise has no alternative and has no money or authority to install additional equipment or to update existing equipment. Various reports confirm the weaknesses in the economic management system: lathes still encased in crates remaining in front of a factory for two to three years; a complete set of equipment to make steel tubes for the Ma-anshan steel plant which remained in a warehouse with the crate unopened for sixteen years; a watch assembly plant constructed and not put in operation because the plant could not adapt to the screw-making techniques at the factory. (72)

There is no incentive in the system to make the most efficient use of inventory and thus large quantities of raw materials may remain unused and stored in warehouses. Since the manufacturing project getting official approval is guaranteed a profit by the central government, there is no relation between production and marketing so it makes little difference if the product meets market demand or if it ends up being stored in a warehouse unsold and unused.

Efficiency is not promoted by the labor system in which the worker lacks freedom of choice for his occupation and is merely assigned to his work. There is little incentive or interest displayed by the worker in production under such a system.

The Chinese leadership in discussing modernization talks of restructuring the economic system. It requires a change in the administrative measures used to manage the economy and to learn from capitalist societies to adjust the economy to respond to market conditions. As China seems to move toward modernization, it is becoming clear to the leadership that there are serious problems in the operation of the socialist economy. After researching the economic system in China, University of California (Berkeley) China expert Chalmers Johnson reported:

> Socialism has failed in China. Although not without any successes at all, socialism has not been able to deliver the rates of development that are dictated by the socioeconomic characteristics of China, nor has it come close to achieving peace in a socialist commonwealth of nations. More particularly, the strenuously sought goal of a "new socialist man," one moved not by material interests but by an ideal, is the most conspicuous failure of them all. . . Socialism provides no more sound a basis for international order than it does for domestic development. (73)

The "China Market": Myth or Reality?

While China would be seeking science and technology from the United States, the idea of a vast "China Market" which would be opened to U.S. businessmen has been used as a lure to gain support for a policy of increased commercial contact with the People's Republic of China. Since the Chinese economy is backward and lacking essentials for a modern industrial economy, the idea is presented as the pot of gold at the end of the rainbow: United States businessmen must be willing to take the long range investment in China so that *someday* a great boom in China trade would occur and one billion Chinese would be suddenly made a part of the "American consumer market."

Realistic observers of the international scene prefer to look at some concrete statistics and historical lessons before rushing into such an optimistic conclusion. Despite the optimistic forecasts by the present Chinese leadership, China's economy yields a total GNP (Gross National Product) of four hundred billion (U.S. dollars) or, considering its population of about one billion people, a per capita GNP yield of four hundred U.S. dollars. It is one fourth the size of the United States economy. (74) China does want something concrete from the United States and other Free World nations, namely advanced science and technology (including knowledge and hardware) in such fields as physics, lasers, petrochemicals, and automation. It is clear that China wants to avoid accepting the culture and society of the Western nations and wishes to remain a nation continuing its social and political revolution. (75) It is clear in this context that two obstacles remain to the idea of China becoming a great customer and a great ally of the United States: 1) the future stability of the government in power is unsure and government leaders and policies could be changed virtually overnight, and 2) China's goals may be too ambitious for its resources as it seeks to follow a policy which could be summed up in the phrase: "Everything has to be done at once." (76)

American rhetoric and actions on China make clear that the argument of the "China Market" has a strong place in policy formulations. When President Jimmy Carter announced on December 15, 1978 that the United States was taking the step of normalizing relations with the People's Republic of China, the idea of trade and the trading potential was used as a selling point. The Carter announcement included a major change in U.S. policy: a derecognition of the government of the Republic of China on Taiwan as the legitimate government of the Chinese people and the recognition of a government in control of the mainland of China which the United States had not extended recognition since its takeover of China in October of 1949. The U.S. President stated that recognition would be extended to the PRC on January 1, 1979, and the U.S. liaison office in Peking and the PRC liaison office in the U.S. would be raised to embassy level on March 1, 1979. (The United States, as part of the derecognition of Taiwan, gave notice that the mutual defense treaty between the U.S. and the Republic of China on Taiwan, adopted in 1954, would be formally terminated January 1, 1980.) (77)

It had taken about ten years of activity to bring about this result. Secretary of State Henry Kissinger had paved the way with his visit to Peking in the summer of 1971. This led to the visit to Peking by President Richard M. Nixon in February of 1972 and the issuance of the Shanghai Communique in February 28, 1972, an ambiguous statement stating the respective positions of the People's Republic of China and the United

States on the "China Question." Liaison offices were opened in Washington, D.C. and Peking in May of 1973. The National Council for U.S.-China Trade was formed and trade between the United States and China began to expand. It was declared that it would be "the policy of the U.S. Government to promote trade in nonstrategic goods with the PRC." (78)

President Carter's announcement of diplomatic relations with the PRC came as a surprise to many observers. Officials in Taiwan were not notified until that morning of this massive change in U.S. policy. While noting that the U.S. intended to continue strong trade and cultural relations with Taiwan, he also welcomed "a new vista for properous trade relations with almost a billion people in the People's Republic of China." (79)

Other Carter Administration spokesmen followed the same theme. Secretary of State Cyrus Vance stressed that diplomatic relations between the two nations could lead to the structure necessary for exchanges in science and trade. He cited the economic benefits particularly:

> These include our participation as a regular supplier of agricultural commodities to China, the ability of U.S. exporters to compete on an equal basis with other suppliers, and the resumption of shipping, air, banking, and other normal economic relations with China. (80)

Then Secretary of Commerce Juanita M. Kreps pointed to China's "ambitious modernization plans for industry and agriculture" which called for one hundred twenty key projects in addition to the upgrading of selected existing facilities. She gained additional optimism from evaluating the total market size of China and the clear indication that China's leadership was interested in importing foreign technology and equipment: China, based on its planned goals, would be likely to import fifty billion (U.S. dollars) of complete plant equipment and the full capital equipment bill might run as high as between seventy to eighty five billion (U.S. dollars) in the period 1978-1985. She added that the United States exports to the PRC could total ten billion (U.S. dollars) over the next five years.(81)

W. Michael Blumenthal, then U.S. Secretary of the Treasury, pointed to an "opening to the West" in China in which Western governments and private enterprise could take advantage of numerous commercial opportunities. He predicted that the United States has the opportunity to create new and vital economic ties with a China that is bent on entering the front ranks of the world's economic powers by the end of the century (82).

The United States government moved quickly to open the door to the "China Market." In July of 1979, the United States and China signed a comprehensive trade agreement, less than six months after the normalization of diplomatic relations between the two nations. The agreement was expected to increase U.S. involvement in China's development especially in oil exploration and the development of iron ore and other mining facilities. The trade pact, which would have to be approved by the U.S. Congress, would reduce high tariff barriers against Chinese goods, allowing China to export goods to the United States at a lower price since tariffs would drop from an average of twenty-four per cent to five per cent, a rate paid by other countries. One stumbling block to trade relations had been reached in early 1979 on U.S. property claims against China and Chinese counterclaims on assets frozen in the U.S. (83) The three year agreement with China would grant China "most favored nation" status, a completely nondiscriminatory treatment to China regarding trade. (84)

The early prospects for a greatly expanding trade with Mainland China and United States businessmen, so bright in January of 1979, began definitely fading within six months, notably about the time of the trade agreement signing. Juanita Krebs, then U.S. Secretary of Commerce, returned from a mid-year trip to China stating on her return that any growth in U.S.-China trade would be gradual and at a much slower rate than had been anticipated. An Asian newspaper, *The China Post*, editorialized that Secretary Kreps' prediction was "the understatement of the year" and added:

> In 1978 American sales to Red China were worth US$824 million. The United States purchased from the mainland: cotton, shirts, tin, feathers, fireworks and peanuts worth US$324 million. It added up to a two-way total of US$1.2 billion. By contrast American trade with the Republic of China was valued at US$ 7.4 billion, making the Republic of China America's eight largest trading partner. The estimated two way trade with Red China this year is about

US$1.7 billion. The projected trade with the Republic of China is more than US$9 billion. (85)

The China Post editorial noted that there were many reasons why trade with Mainland China was not promising. While China occupies the third largest land mass in the world (after the Soviet Union and Canada), that only one-fifth of China's land is arable and eighty per cent of the population is engaged in subsistence farming. China's distribution system (e.g., rail transport) has serious deficiencies as well as the operation of its industrial economic system. For example, when the Chinese leadership ordered the steel industry to double its production by 1985, production during 1978 went up by about seven million tons but investments were diverted from other areas and the extra electricity needed resulted in a fall in production in other plants by fifty per cent. It summarized the problem of U.S.-China trade:

> If Peiking hopes to expand its imports to the United States, the prospect is dim . . . there is a limit to the quantity of rice wine, pickled bamboo shoots and ginseng roots the American market wants. The only profitable export of Communist China is narcotics; and the United States receives most of the dope traffic against its will. President Carter prefers to ignore that item in the trade with Red China. (86)

The People's Republic of China is anxious to find willing partners in its program to get needed technology. During 1979, China made contracts with the United States, West Germany, Japan, France, Italy, Sweden, Australia, Canada, and Argentina totaling about $30 billion. The adoption of the statute for "joint operation of enterprises with foreign investors" in July of 1979 has been a lure to enhance international cooperation and technical interflow. Yet, the lessons of the sudden suspension of the contracts should not be lost on other nations who may put too much reliance on the words and promises of Mainland China. As one newspaper in Asia noted, the suspension of purchase contracts by Peking "had not only rocked the business world in Japan but also shocked the economic communities in Europe and the United States." (87) Those businessmen who believe it will happen to businessmen of other nations and not to them may be in for a major surprise.

The United States especially needs to take a realistic view of China trade in the past and in the future. The economy of the People's Republic of China is the sixth largest in the world following that of the United States, the Soviet Union, Japan, West Germany, and France. While China is a ranking economic power, its economic status does not correspond to its population size (e.g., the largest nation in the world with between twenty to twenty-five per cent of the world's population) nor does it compare to the world's economic giants. China's exports have not exceeded two percent of the world's total while its total trade is the lowest of any nation in Asia and the lowest of any major nation, between five to six per cent of its GNP. When considering trade on a per capita basis, China averages about fourteen (U.S.) dollars per person and near the bottom of all nations in the world. China has been actively working to increase its trade and dealings with capitalist countries. However, historically, China has never been an important United States trading partner and American trade with China never constituted more than two per cent of total United States trade. These facts are part of the historical record even when the United States at the time of the "Open Door" policy sought to keep China "open" for trade around the turn of the century and at the time of close commercial and political relations with the government of Chiang Kai-shek on Mainland China in the 1930's and 1940's. During the latter period cited, U.S. share of the China trade varied between fifteen and nineteen per cent. Even if the United States could gain a similar share of trade with China – which seems unlikely even to the most optimistic forecasters – U.S.-China trade would still be less than America's present trade with South Korea or Hong Kong and only a fraction of U.S. trade with the Republic of China on Taiwan .(88) Even if China restructures its trade with the United States by a significant margin, it seems unlikely that there would be any more than a total of one billion (U.S.) dollars to two billion (U.S.) dollars in two way trade in the 1980's, a rather low figure for the United States. (89)

It appears that China may have achieved its highest volume of trade feasible for the near future for the following reasons: China's huge size makes for a large internal market; the planned Chinese economy makes planners prefer domestic trade over international trade; a shift in leadership and programs may reduce the current emphasis on international commercial contacts. (90)

Experts note that serious limitations on increasing trade fall into four categories: both countries (the U.S. and China) have self-sufficient economies; there are serious obstacles to China importing technology, technology-intensive goods, and weapons from the United States; China has little the United States needs and must compete with other developing countries in the market; China lacks foreign exchange to pay for U.S. imports and, while needing to sell more abroad, China's export potential is seriously limited. (91)

China does desire heavy industrial and technological equipment as well as agricultural commodities. The question still remains how China will finance its efforts at modernization since the PRC lacks adequate foreign reserves, accumulation of vast revenues from oil exportation is unlikely, and the few export commodities of the PRC face strong competition in world markets. (92) A report from the Office of Technology Assessment, an arm of the U.S. Congress, reported on this Chinese reliance on the West:

> China's imports from the West have been crucial to the development of key industrial sectors such as steel and petrochemicals. China's modernization drive, although significantly less ambitious now than as originally announced in February 1978, depends on imports of plant and associated technology to play an important role in strengthening the industrial infrastructure, raising productivity in the agricultural sector, and in the exploration and development of energy resources. (93)

A strictly economic interpretation may find a ready immediate market in China for certain technology like computers and even military weapons. Opposition, however, is likely to arise within the United States to such sales as well as from

United States allies and even the Soviet Union. China's recent actions against Vietnam alarmed the world community. Two experts on Asia, William R. Kintner, former U.S. Ambassador to Thailand, and John F. Copper, Associate Professor in International Studies at Southwestern University in Memphis, Tennessee and widely traveled in Asia, raised a crucial point in a recent publication:

> Washington must always consider the possibility of China using American technology or weapons against an Asian neighbor, especially one allied with the United States. The fact that Soviet weapons sold to China in the 1950's are aimed at Russian cities is a vivid example of this dilemma. (94)

Trade between the U.S. and the PRC may never achieve a stable basis because of the instability of trade in a planned economy and of the poor performances of China's economy in the past. In China's planned economy, imports are part of a policy in order to ease pressure on the domestic transport and distribution system (especially supplying grain to coast cities), correct planning errors as a result of poor harvests and underinvestment in some sectors, and accelerate economic growth by importing capital goods that China cannot produce itself. (95)

As pointed out before, the U.S. trade with the Republic of China on Taiwan (and Asian nations like Japan and South Korea) is much more impressive and stable than the promise of trade with the People's Republic of China. Although reflecting a hostility toward the movement of the United States toward the People's Republic of China, Premier Sun Yun-suan of the Republic of China on Taiwan, spoke before the annual dinner of the American Chamber of Commerce in Taiwan a month after the Carter Administration announcement on diplomatic ties with the PRC. He urged businessmen "not to be taken in" by the Chinese Communists who desire U.S. help to finance the "four modernizations." In a friendly but stern warning of the path ahead, Premier Sun attempted to highlight some of the problems of trading with Communist China:

> Mainland China is one of the most backward of Com-

> munist lands. Those who think the Chinese are going to accept the American business community as a full-fledged partner do not understand the realities. The Chinese Communists will take but they will not give. There is no mainland "market" of 900 million people. Per capita income of a few hundred dollars a year is barely sufficient for a subsistence diet and patched clothing. 80% of the people still depend on agriculture for existence and Hu Chiao Mu himself has stated that per capita production of food grains was the same in 1977 as it was in 1955. The power and transportation systems are woefully inadequate for even the present low level of industry. Electricity use in Canton is limited to ten kwh monthly per household. Successful economic development depends on a steady continuity of constructive, responsive policy over a long period. The ongoing cycle of purge and revenge on the mainland will not, and cannot, achieve such an environment. (96)

The "China Market" is not an entity to be easily captured by mere access to the People's Republic of China and may well be, from historical experience, a "myth" which may bring more disadvantages in the long run than advantages. American and Western businessmen need to approach with care and to understand the full ramifications of trade with Communist China.

Practical Problems of "Doing Business" With China

Aside from the problem of ascertaining the significance of the China Market, there are a number of practical problems which face the American and Western businessman when dealing with the People's Republic of China. Some of these difficulties stem from the cultural and business practices of both nations. Other problems result from the Chinese Communist economy and its lack of a sound pricing or trade mechanism. Other difficulties may arise from the Communists seeking to get the best deal possible in trade while following the practices they demand be followed.

The Canton Fair illustrates some of the problems faced by

the businessman seeking to get involved in the "China Market." The biannual Canton Trade Fairs, first opening in 1956, have served as a means for China to have commercial contacts with other nations and provided an opportunity for other countries to have business contact with China. (97) The Chinese control the event very tightly. Stanley Young, vice president of the National Council for U.S.-China Trade, stated that twenty thousand American businessmen wanted to come to the Canton Fair in October but only seven hundred received the necessary invitations. The uncertainty of the China trade market can be revealed at the fair: the previous autumn China purchased chemicals from U.S. firms worth eighty million (U.S. dollars) while during the following spring fair the China purchases plummeted to only twenty-six million (U.S. dollars). Prices were also much higher at the spring fair. China promoted a number of its goods including arts and crafts, native products, light industrial goods, minerals and metals. (98)

American businessmen have complained that an enforced long stay at the Canton Fair, due to Chinese practices, cause them to lose other economic opportunities for profit elsewhere and, unless large orders are placed, they are not invited back. These businessmen must deal with intermediaries (e.g., State Trading Agency) rather than "end users" and cannot deal with the "end users" who eventually buy and use the product; they lose that type of direct contact to find what the customer actually needs and what would be the most beneficial price for both parties concerned. As far as the Chinese products offered, the market designs of Chinese products are inflexible and the Chinese are not familiar with the Western pricing system (e.g., the Chinese attempt to sell items for the same price to retailers and wholesalers). The output of some Chinese products are exceptionally small and limited and thus prohibit some buyers from buying large quantities. The international payment mechanism (e.g., the Chinese prefer the letter of credit) causes inconveniencies and ties up capital for the American businessman. The change in the foreign exchange rate can leave one party at an economic disadvantage. The purchaser from the United States or Western Europe has little recourse even if he has received defective goods since the final word on the matter is the decision by the Chinese Bureau of Commodity Inspection which certifies whether Chinese export shipments meet specifications. The Chinese, on the other hand, can enforce a penalties clause in their contract if goods from a purchaser are delayed. (99)

The U.S. Department of Commerce has suggested that companies be prepared to spend a full year negotiating an initial transaction with the Chinese Communists. One gets to do business with the Chinese only by invitation and China prefers to do business with "old friends"; thus there is priority on establishing a long term contact. China's own uncertainty on how fast it wants to modernize and in what sectors has led to delays and postponements on contracts supposedly agreed to by parties earlier. Overall, it is clear that China will not even come close to spending the six hundred billion (U.S. dollars) for modernization by 1985 which had been so widely discussed at the time of normalization. (100)

China has taken action to lure additional contacts for trade. When Mao Tse-tung ruled China, the Bank of China had to keep imports and exports in approximate balance and it was not allowed to accept foreign loans. This policy was changed in 1978 and presently the Bank of China seems to employ whatever banking practice which will accelerate China's ambitious development program. At the trade fair, fairgoers for the first time are able to use East Asia Bank Americard-Visa cards for purchases. The Bank of China has established two investment banks as well. As the end of 1979 approached, the People's Republic of China thru its Bank of China accounted for about one-seventh of the Exim Bank credits and ten to fifteen per cent of the loans on the Eurocurrency market. It is clear that the Chinese leadership is still maintaining strong control of economic organs. In April of 1979, the Bank of China came under tighter control by central planners and was placed directly under the State Council instead of the People's Bank of China, its former parent body. The State Council also directs a State General Administration of Exchange Control, a form of exchequer of the country's foreign exchange reserves and watchdog over the Bank of China's international payments. (101)

Considering China's limited foreign exchange, it may be possible that China may have to move toward barter in some of its trade dealings. Some American companies have shown interest in barter, a two way trade of commodities using a single contract without exchange of money but details are scarce on how and if such arrangements can be made. China has had product for product exchange trade with Pakistan and signed similar type agreements (e.g. commodity exchange agreements with Asian, African and Latin American nations.) It seems likely that Peking will be pressuring foreign companies to find ways of exchanging product for product. (102) It is difficult to find how this could bring about much significant trade between the United States and China since China has few products which the U.S. needs.

One of the proposed trade deals between China and the U.S. which illustrates some of the real difficulties concerns the one with McDonnell Douglas Corporation calling for the purchase by China of a number of the company's jets and the joint production arrangement between the U.S. and China. In the McDonnell Douglas Corporation proposal, China would buy some aircraft outright but would likely buy the minimum number to upgrade its fleet of domestic airliners. The other part of the deal includes Chinese technicians actually assembling the planes or parts of the planes in Shanghai with parts being shipped in from the United States. The manner in which this tranfer of technology will take place has to be worked out. It is unlikely it will be through a joint venture. Part of the package may be thru a "compensation trade" agreement, a form of barter with the Chinese buying technology and paying for it in kind rather than in cash. It has been suggested, for example, that China may pay for coal mining equipment with coal or sewing machines with shirts. In the McDonnell Douglas case, it is unlikely that China will be able to pay with the specimens of DC9's and thus no agreement has been reached on the form of the exchange. (103)

While it is true that the major nations which recognized the People's Republic of China thru formal diplomatic relations experienced immediate increased trade between their nation and the PRC, it is also true that this did not result in a continuous increase. Despite the difficulties cited in dealing with China on trade, nations such as Japan, Australia, France and West Germany found that trade benefits accruing to them depending heavily on the overall direction of Chinese foreign policy and on the state of political stability and the economic needs of China. During the turmoil of the Cultural Revolution, countries with diplomatic and trade linkages to China found these more of a liability than an advantage. (104) There are definite difficulties in establishing a stable trade relationship with the People's Republic of China since internal politics play such a large role in their trading policies and there is always the uncertainty of how long a trade relationship will last since a quick change in policy could abruptly terminate an ongoing trade policy. The modernization program itself may bring about tensions and economic dislocations and contradictions which might serious limit the actualization of this program. (105)

China's Modernization: What Significance for the Future?

Having considered some of the problems inherent in the "China Market" and some of the practical problems of doing business with China, there are some international aspects of providing the People's Republic of China with Western technology and science. These are important considerations for the type of world the United States and the Free World hope to face in future years.

Consideration should be given to whether China can achieve its modernization objectives and at what price for the United States, Japan, and the Western World. The nations which are willing to trade with China must be prepared for overpromising – and for then sudden cancellations of contracts. As for other issues, trade with Communist China requires a consideration of relations with the Soviets, the human rights question, and future relations with the Republic of China on Taiwan. Finally, if China achieves "modernization," industrialization, and development, and if it receives these benefits thru Western technology, what role will a strong and industrial China play in world politics?

A thorough consideration of the problems, difficulties, and weaknesses in the Chinese economy, especially industry is needed. The attempt to complete the "four modernizations" – agriculture, industry, national defense, science and technology – by the end of the century appears to be an impossible achievement. More realistic statements have attempted to make China's goal for the end of the century the level Japan had reached in the 1970's, a twenty to thirty year slideback from the originally announced goals. (106)

The Chinese may take a number of actions to reach their modernization goals including shortening the time of capital construction, reform and straighten out the existing enterprises, close down or suspend those enterprises which have suffered losses for a long time, and revamp the economic management system. Yet, there is the problem that readjustment could cause an economic slump in the Chinese economy which would result in economic as well as political stability problems. Communist ideology will permit only certain developments in casting aside the socialist system in China.

The Chinese Communists must continue to deal with the slowdown in production in agriculture as well as overpopulation and unemployment. They have attempted to remedy the problems of lack of capital, substandard technology, inefficient management, a shortage of scientists and technicians, and the lack of modern technology and equipment by seeking aid from abroad. The Chinese Communists will seek to rely on Japan and the Western nations in the 1980's as they relied on the Soviets to rebuild their economy in the 1950's and lay the basis for an industrial society.

Despite numerous problems, the Chinese industrial structure is stronger today than when they first established their regime on the mainland in 1949. If China is successful in securing a large amount of aid from the industrially advanced countries of the Western world, this nation may achieve greater progress in industry than was possible by accepting Soviet aid in the 1950's. However, many of these same Western nations, as well as the United States, may wonder what is the long range price of helping China with technology and development aid to build itself into a strong world power in the 1980's and beyond. Will these countries gain monetarily from more trade or will they be building up a powerful adversary power in world politics for a future confrontation?

Despite the adoption of a science development plan for China for 1985, experts have stated that the plan seems overly optimistic and may take China more than fifty years to catch up considering the great economic costs involved. (107)

One Asian observer noted that Communist China to achieve its ambitious goals must sell more of its products (especially oil and other natural resources) in order to buy technology from Japan, the United States and other Western countries. That export promotion is likely to be a very difficult business for the Chinese Communists. These difficulties in future years may come from protectionism in Western nations because of a slowdown in economic growth in these Western nations and the need for China to devote more of its output to the domestic market as its economy keeps growing. (108) A perceptive American observer, Professor Edward N. Luttwak, then associate director of the Washington Center of Foreign Policy Research at Johns Hopkins University, visited the People's Republic of China in 1976 and wrote on the waste of resources he observed while on his travels. He wrote that even the most casual exposure to China would disapprove the notion that a person was dealing with an "emergent superpower" and, except for its nuclear power, China lacks all the attributes of a superpower. He speculated that there was doubt in his mind that China could become such a superpower even in the next thirty years. Turning to the economic inefficiencies, he concluded on China's status:

> The total cost of such irrationality in the few hundred factories and power plants that make up the island of modern industry in the sea of China's primitive economy is obviously the root cause of the slow growth of the Chinese economy, where the heavy sacrifices of the masses are in large part squandered by the gross mismanagement of the provincial and central planners. To be sure, Chinese industrial growth has been of the order of 7 per cent a

> year since the chaotic disruptions of the Cultural Revolution came to an end. And this does compare very well with Western rates of growth. But on the very small base-level of Chinese industry it does not amount to much. More significant, it is a much *lower* rate of growth than in Hong Kong, Singapore, or Taiwan. If present trends continue, China will become the backward country cousin of these other Chinese economies. As of now the Chinese economy is downright medieval compared to that of South Korea, let alone Japan. (109)

Reference has already been made to the possible disappointments inherent in the "China fever" with the experience of Japan being the key example of cancelled and suspended contracts. Japan and China had signed an eight year bilateral trade agreement (February, 1978) which called for each country to export ten billion (U.S. dollars) worth of goods and knowhow to each other. Japan would provide industrial plants and other manufactured items while China would export coal, oil, and other commodities. By January of 1979, Japan had sold China about four and half billion (U.S. dollars) worth of thirty-five large scale industrial plants, nearly half of Japan's total plant exports for 1978. Although China's foreign currency reserves are estimated to be only between two billion to three billion (U.S. dollars), China in one year alone had signed with Japanese and Western firms for a total of seven billion (U.S. dollars) worth of business! China deferred these contracts because it could not afford to pay for them. Newspaper writer Yasuhiko Sagara, writing in the *Asahi Journal* in Japan, put the lessons from this experience as follows:

> The business community had caught "China fever." It was no psychosomatic illusion; there was ample reason to be excited about the China market.
>
> But if Japanese businessmen thought the Chinese would continue signing contracts indefinitely, "China fever" had impaired their judgment. . . Dreams of great increase in trade with China have been replaced by a mood of distrust. (110)

As for increasing trade, the United States and Western

nations should be aware that China has used trade as a means of accomplishing political objectives such as using oil exports to encourage Japan to establish diplomatic relations with the People's Republic of China and using the promise to import large quantities of steel to encourage the signing of the Sino-Japanese Peace Treaty. China later suspended these same contracts made with Japan. (111)

One of the factors involved in U.S. aid to China has been the effect on U.S. relations with the Soviet Union. Some observers believe both powers are hostile to the U.S. and that the U.S. should not aid either to gain militarily or economically since the strength and power will be used one day against the United States and the Free World. Others seek to woo China, and use it as a counterweight and ally against the Soviets. Still others seek to please both powers and grant "most favored nation" treatment to both Communist powers. (112) Despite the emphasis on civilian exchange with China, there have been rumors of China being interested in U.S. military planes and associated technology. (113) There is a temptation that building up China militarily may require Soviet Russia to station more troops on the Sino-Soviet border and thus helping to relieve pressure on Europe. Brian Crozier, columnist and expert on international affairs, noted that a military tie-up between the U.S. and China or the Western nations and China is extremely fragile and risky since China's perceptions of its interest is based on ideology and China can change its entire orientation based on the whim of a Communist party boss in charge. (114) During a period of delicate international relations, it may be necessary to proceed with caution in dealing with both Communist powers rather than to risk a dubious strategy attempting to play one off against the other. Although there is a rivalry between the two nations, both Soviet Russia and Communist China are essentially hostile to the democracy, capitalism, and political freedom existing in the societies of the Free World. As to playing the "China card," Professor Edward N. Luttwak has observed:

> Hence the right-wing Sinophilia of those who abhor the Chinese system but who see virtue in Chinese power as a

counterweight to the Russian, is as flawed as the left-wing Sinophilia of those who see virtue in a society which combines a maximum of unfreedom with a minimum of efficiency. (115)

China can always use any renewed military strength on military adventures in Asia – either where there is Sino-Soviet rivalry (e.g., Vietnam, Cambodia) or where there are non-Communist Asian states (e.g., Thailand, South Korea, the Republic of China on Taiwan).

If Soviet Russia and Communist China reach an accommodation and join forces, any remembrance of gratitude to the United States or the Western world will be shortlived as both powers seek to bring additional Communist states into existence.

Preliminary discussion of the U.S. granting "most favored nation" (MFN) treatment to the People's Republic of China immediately hit two obstacles. The first was in textiles with a strong push to limit China's imports to the U.S. The White House promised Congress it would act through its unilateral quota power to secure a reduction in Communist China's shipment of clothing and textile goods to the U.S. A second obstacle was concern over the willingness of China to allow its people to emigrate freely. The U.S. State Department said it had oral assurances from Chinese officials that such a policy was in effect. (116)

The promise to limit China's textiles to the U.S. is tenuous at best. The United States imports large amounts of textile products from its Asian allies (e.g. South Korea, the Republic of China on Taiwan) and it is unlikely that the U.S. needs additional textile products from Mainland China. The People's Republic of China could easily pressure the U.S. to accept more textile goods as a "barter arrangement" for technology and can use this pressure as a means to undermine the market in textiles for U.S. allies by underselling the economies of non-Communist Asian states.

Since trade with the Soviets on "most favored nation" (MFN) status has been tied to human rights and emigration policies (e.g., Jackson-Vanik amendment), it would be difficult to establish a separate standard, or a special exemption, for Communist China. The trial and sentencing to fifteen years in prison of Wei Jingsheng, accused of passing military secrets to foreign reporters and having engaged in counterrevolutionary activities, has raised most recently the question of the status of human rights in China. Wei was quoted in the trial as saying that the situation in China was no different than when the "gang of four" ruled China. (117) Amy Young-Anwaty, Executive Director of the International Human Rights Law Group, a public interest law firm seeking to promote international human rights law and procedures, urged caution in granting "most favored nation" status to China stressing that insistence on respect for human rights should be a *quid pro quo* for trade benefits for China before the trade agreement is implemented. The spokesman noted that news accounts and Amnesty International had indicated that human rights were in a precarious state in China. (118) A special report prepared by the Far Eastern Law Division of the Library of Congress for the United States Senate Committee on Foreign Relations noted that since the ousting of the "gang of four" the human rights situation in China compares unfavorably with that of the citizens of Western democracies and will likely continue to do so in the future. The report noted that the Chinese great liberality for emigration was tied more to winning "most favored nation" treatment from the United States and winning the support of Overseas Chinese rather than a real concern for human rights. (119) Amnesty International has complained that all of its approaches to Communist China about death sentences and individual cases of prisoners of conscience have remained unanswered. Restricted access to information and lack of official statistics have made it difficult to even estimate the number of prisoners of conscience imprisoned. During one of the most recent reports, the organization noted that during 1977 and 1978 there were continued purges and arrests of cadres in China as being linked to the "gang of four." (120) If the United States intends to make "human rights" a consideration of its foreign policy, it cannot exclude China from following the basic requirements which it requires of other nations. It is an aspect of China's policy which cannot be ignored if the U.S. is to be consistent in its concern with the conditions of citizens in other nations.

As U.S. and Western businessmen look toward the "China Market" on the mainland, they must also consider a strong and viable "China Market" in operation in the Republic of China on Taiwan. The ROC had a remarkable 12.8 per cent real growth in 1978 and, despite the large increase in oil prices and the slowdown in economic growth of Taiwan's leading trade partners (notably the United States), it achieved a real growth rate in 1979 of eight per cent and will likely be in excess of eight per cent annually in the next five years. During the past twenty years, Taiwan has experienced an average growth rate of nine per cent annually and has served as a good example in economic development for other developing nations. The growth in the average yearly income in Taiwan has increased from $148 in 1952 to $1079 in 1977 and reached about $1750 in 1979. Foreign and overseas investment in Taiwan since 1952 has exceeded 2.2 billion (U.S. dollars); the United States has over five hundred million (U.S. dollars) invested in Taiwan with a very profitable return. Investment applications approved by the ROC in 1979 totaled about three hundred million (U.S. dollars). The best estimates are that Taiwan's GNP reached thirty billion (U.S. dollars) in 1979. (121)

While the suddeness of the U.S. announcement on normalization of relations with Mainland China sent shock waves through the government and economic leadership on Taiwan, events in Taipei have returned to normal and the normalization decision by the U.S. has not disrupted Taiwan's economic growth. The United States remains the largest economic partner of Taiwan as well as the most important guarantor of its security. (122)

The People's Republic of China claims Taiwan as part of its territory and has expressed its intention to unify China. The leadership in Taiwan has made it clear that it will not abandon its freedom and sovereignty to become united with the mainland while a Communist regime rules it. As the People's Republic of China increases its economic and military strength, it may renew its call more forcefully for such a unification and may use more subtle means to undermine the economy of Taiwan (e.g., underselling Taiwan on world markets, pressure on foreign business to trade with the PRC rather than the ROC). Taiwan with a strong military and with continuing economic prosperity will remain in a strong position to resist such pressure if this island nation is not undermined by its allies, particularly the United States.

Much of the future of the two Chinas depends on how the major powers, especially the United States and Japan, react to the future developments in Asia. After normalization, there was concern in Asia over the ramification of such a change in U.S. policy. Caution over the future is still the watchword.(123) Peking has shown that it can bring strong trade, diplomatic, and political pressures to achieve its objectives. In the past, the leadership in Peking sought to break up Japan-Taiwan air traffic, brought pressure on Japan to bar ROC ships in its ports, and worked to have Chinese residing in Japan switch their loyalty (e.g., passports) from the government in Taipei to the government in Peking. The Chinese Communists have only experienced limited success but are likely to continue trying to undermine Taiwan via economic pressures on other nations. (124)

A major question is how the United States, Japan, and the Western European powers will respond in the future to Mainland China's attempts to use trade as a political weapon against Taiwan and other nations. If there is concern over this policy of Peking, the United States and other Free World nations must use caution in providing China with advanced technology, science, and agricultural products. If these powers rush in without any reasonable assurances of Peking's peaceful uses of its technology and aim only for cash values or sales contracts, they may find disappointment. They may find that China will not pay the money promised through suspension or cancellation of contracts. Even worse, they may find that they have built up a nation economically and militarily that might be a rival in trade or an adversary in international relations. The United States, for example, would need to develop a policy which would prevent overextension of credits while assuring that the viable "China Market" in Taiwan will not be endangered. (125)

On the basis of strict competition, the economy of the

Republic of China on Taiwan is far ahead of that of Mainland China in skilled labor, sound management, established trade relations, and a sound track record of stability and reliability.(126) A spirit of optimism and confidence is evident by the officials of the government of Taiwan despite the outreach of Mainland China to the Western nations. The Director of the Department of Mainland Affairs of the Kuomintang Central Committee on Taiwan, Pai Wong-hsiang has observed:

> Just as the Soviet Union cannot catch up with the United States in economic development, Red China will not be able to match free China. The basic reason lies in the different economic systems. The Chinese mainland can never catch up with the Republic of China unless the Peiping regime gives up its Communist economic system, abolishes the "people's communes" and returns property to the people. (127)

As the 1980's open, the actions of the People's Republic of China will require intensive scutiny. There are definite changes occurring. The Chinese Communists realize that if they are going to be trading with the Western nations they need to modernize their ports and they do show a great interest in learning as much as possible about the latest shipping and cargo handling techniques. (128) The Chinese have planned to dispatch two officials to take a crash course in an American law firm in the field of American law to better grasp the intricacies of legal codes and rules on trade and foreign investment. (129) China has been seeking to send large teams of migrant workers to Arab nations in order to earn hard currency and gain valuable experience as well as winning friends for China. Projects would include construction and public works such as buildings, roads and airports; the chief countries under consideration would be Iran, Kuwait, Libya, and the United Arab Emirates (UAE).(130) In July of 1978, China had nearly six million students take a standardized test in eight areas (politics, history, geography, mathematics, physics, chemistry, Chinese language, and one foreign language with a choice from English, French, Spanish, Russian, German, Japanese, or Arabic); five per cent of the students were selected to go on for advanced training. This was the first such standardized test given in China since the Cultural Revolution began in 1966. (131)

The more things change, the more they remain the same. China seems likely to purchase from Britain Harrier jumpjet aircraft with Rolls Royce likely to supply China with the technology to build advanced jet engines for fighter aircraft. A four nation tour (France, West Germany, Britain, and Italy) by Hua Kuo-feng in November of 1979 turned out to be a disappointment for exporters in these above mentioned nations since the Chinese were doing little buying. Since Britain hosted about one hundred twenty technical missions from China during eleven months of 1979, some British critics were saying that these missions were turning out to be little more than missions to examine equipment or a means of getting cheap consulting advice without any intention to buy. (132). The watchword for the 1980's may be the cautious approach which some foreign investors were making based on observation and experience. Derek Davies, editor of *The Far Eastern Economic Review*, has stated the case as follows:

> Many (investors) have been counting up the relatively small returns gained so far on the expenditure of a lot of time, effort and money on exploring projects which were never realized or tendering for schemes which went to competitors willing to offer giveaway prices and concessional terms on finance. . . The reassessment has mitigated much of the over-ambitious zeal on the part of China's own economic officials, but the delays of the past year have also dissipated the euphoria which until recently flushed the cheeks of American, European and Japanese businessmen and bankers. (133)

As for the United States, the issue reached a national forum when the U.S. Congress considered on January 24, 1980 President Carter's request to extend "Most-Favored-Nation" (MFN) treatment to the People's Republic of China. While proponents of the legislation used the standard arguments that such a policy would assist U.S. businessmen in trade, would aid the improvement of U.S.-China relations, and would serve as an attempt to build a counter to the Soviets, critics focused on the poor record of Communist China in paying debts, the harmful consequences such trade could bring to U.S. industries and its trade with allies, and the totalitarian nature of the ruling Chinese government.

Major opposition was led by House Ways and Means Committee Member, Representative Richard T. Schulze of Pennsylvania. Observing that he did not oppose increased trade between the United States and the People's Republic of China, he did express his concern that the extension of "Most-Favored-Nation" status to China would not be in the best interest of the U.S. at this particular time. He pointed out that although recognizing the Carter Administration sought new alliances to offset the Soviet Union's expansionist efforts particularly in Afghanistan, any consideration of improved relations with China needed to be beneficial to both nations and the proposed MFN legislation left many questions unanswered and many issues unresolved.

The Pennsylvania Congressman cited the 23 billion (U.S. dollars) China had available in unused credits and its failure to repay the 50 million (U.S. dollars) it accumulated in defaulted Export-Import Bank loans. Another unresolved issue concerned financial compensation to those Americans who held 220 million (U.S. dollars) in Chinese Government bonds. He cited the precedent that other nations which received MFN status – Hungary, Yugoslavia, Poland, Romania – agreed to pay the debts of their non-Communist predecessor governments before they received MFN status. He queried his colleagues:

> I see no logical reason now to forgive the Chinese Government from its financial responsibilities and believe such misguided generosity would establish a very bad precedent for the future. How can we realistically expect any foreign nation to pay its past debts to the United States when we allow the Chinese to avoid theirs. As elected representatives, do not we have a responsibility to protect the interests of our citizens and to require, as we have in the past, that Chinese settle these financial issues prior to receiving most-favored-nation trade treatment. (134)

Other issues were raised during the debate concerning the direct effect on the United States. The U.S. Treasury estimated MFN would result in lost customs revenues for Fiscal Year 1980 of $47 million and rising to $183 million by fiscal year 1985. Estimates were quoted that MFN status for China would cause a job loss to Americans in certain industries of between fifty thousand to one hundred thousand jobs. Industries affected would be those of textiles, steel, nonrubber footwear, leather, clock-making, and food items such as mushrooms. For example, the Big Ben clock, which sells in the U.S. for $19.95, has a Chinese equivalent which retails in Australia for $4.20; MFN would reduce U.S. duty rates on Chinese clocks from 102 percent to 24 percent. Even without MFN status, the People's Republic of China, paying its workers as little as $35 a month and apprentices $8.50 a month, had aggressively secured a position as the second biggest supplier of cotton gloves taking away 20 per cent of the American market with a substantial erosion of American jobs in the cotton gloves industry; MFN would lower rates on such textiles by 66 per cent. In addition, China would be able to secure loans at the rate of 7 to 8 per cent through subsidized interest rates while U.S. citizens must pay interest rates for loans for automobiles and homes in excess of 15 per cent. (135)

During the discussion of the resolution, other Members of the House of Representatives cited the totalitarian and aggressive nature of both the Chinese Communist government and the Soviet Communist government. Citing the similarity between the two Communist superpowers and warning of the error of building up Communist China as a counter to the Soviets, Ohio Representative John M. Ashbrook asserted:

> I share the deep and sincere concern of my colleagues over the events in Afghanistan and the recognition that major steps must be taken to counter the armored thrusts of the Soviet war machine. However, the last thing this Congress should do is embrace one Communist menace to counter another. The lesson that should have been learned from Afghanistan is that communism is by its very nature aggressive, totalitarian, and militaristic. Whether in the U.S.S.R., in Cuba, or in mainland China the doctrine of Marxist-Leninism ultimately leads to expansionism via guns and tanks. The spector of Soviet might rolling over the people of Afghanistan only proves that the Soviets are more advanced in the tools of adventurism than other Communist powers. This advance being, at least in part, fueled by Western technology transfers. . .
>
> The only difference between the Communist Chinese

and the Soviets is that the Soviets took Kabul first. If we do not stop and reflect before we vote on this measure we may find ourselves standing in this same Chamber 10 or 15 years from now trying to fathom how we allowed ourselves to fuel the arming of China with Western technology.

The Chinese, like other Communists, take an opportunistic stance toward world events. They want their brand of communism to prevail and view the U.S.S.R. as their chief rival. It is in their own best interest to capitalize on the United States' current need for allies and to open their doors to the West. They need industrialization and Western automation to compete with the Soviets. For this long-range need they will foresake any number of short-term acts of aggression. For them time is on their side, and the continued inability of the West to understand their ultimate goal buys them even more time. The bill we have before us today fits perfectly with the Chinese scenario for countering the Soviets and eventually the West. (136)

Representative John H. Rousselot of California stated that China seeks high technology and industrial development from the United States and, after having "picked our brains or used our technology," would treat the U.S. the same as the U.S. had been treated by other dictatorial countries after achieving their objectives. (137) Representative Ron Paul of Texas called attention to the internal persecution of its citizens by China, the expropriation of private property in China, and China's aggressive designs on Tibet, Vietnam, and Taiwan. (138) Tennessee Representative John J. Duncan called the MFN for China a violation of the principle of the Jackson-Vanik Amendment to the Trade Act of 1974 because China does not permit free emigration of its citizens and has not given any public assurances to do so in the future. (139) And Representative Ken Kramer of Colorado cited Russia's alliance with Hitler's Germany to share the spoils of war in the World War II period and then Germany's later attack on Russia; he warned against the U.S. extending MFN to "an armed, militant tyranny" (China) until U.S. policy-makers took time to sort out what the U.S. wished in its future relations with China and to evaluate what the U.S. could gain and lose from such a relationship. (140)

Despite impressive arguments urging caution and possible

detrimental future results from extending MFN to China, the House of Representatives adopted the measure, H.Con.Res. 204, by a vote of 294 to 88. After a more limited debate, the Senate adopted the measure the same day by a vote of 74 to 8. (141)

The allure of the "China market" and the perceived need to build up a counter to the Soviets aided MFN for China. One Asian newspaper commented editorially that the Soviet invasion of Afghanistan and the desire to play the "China card" against the Soviets speeded up the passage of the MFN legislation.(142) Yet, a large majority of both Houses of Congress seemed willing to put aside the warning against allying the U.S. with China which had been given by Dr. Ku Cheng-kang, Honorary Chairman of the World Anti-Communist League, at a gathering in the U.S. Senate Caucus Room on July 17, 1979 commemorating the twentieth anniversary of the Captive Nations Resolution:

> One popular strategic concept demands alliance with the Chinese Communists for the restraint of Russians. This seemingly attractive idea is in fact quite mistaken and dangerous.
>
> The mistake lies in the attempt to unite with a force of enslavement for opposition to another similar force. . . The danger stems from the blurring of demarcation between friend and foe. This loosens the free camp and exposes free nations as targets of individual conquest by the Russian and Chinese communists who are racing hard for hegemony. Even more dangerous is that the two Red powers may at any time join hands for their common communization goal and advance together against the free democratic world. (143)

Leaders of the Republic of China on Taiwan reflected disappointment over the U.S. granting MFN to the People's Republic of China. Just in the first year after the U.S. had granted diplomatic recognition to the PRC, Communist China exercised a new economic impact on Asia as it moved into textiles, electronics, and other labor intensive industries and this threatened similar industries in the Republic of China on Taiwan, South Korea, Hong Kong, and Singapore. Since Mainland China pays its workers only a fraction of what workers can make in the four free Asian economies mentioned, cheaper products have already cut into such industries as textiles and the plastic shoes of Taiwan forcing the free Asian nations to readjust and upgrade their economies. The competition is likely to get even stronger as Communist China seeks to undermine the economies of Taiwan, South Korea, Hong Kong, Singapore and other Asian nations. (144)

The Chinese leadership on Taiwan, nevertheless, appears optimistic. Director-General H.K. Shao of Taiwan's Board of Trade of the Ministry of Economic Affairs expressed the view that MFN would not be a threat to the manufacturers on Taiwan and that the Chinese on Taiwan would be stimulated to develop more competitive products and marketing in the U.S. (145) The ROC trades with over one hundred countries with the United States as its largest market since sales to the U.S. made up thirty-five percent of the ROC's total exports in 1979. U.S.-ROC two way trade in 1979 totaled 9 billion (U.S. dollars), making it America's sixth largest trading partner; Taiwan's two-way foreign trade totaled 30 billion (U.S. dollars) placing it as the world's sixteenth largest exporting nation. Even during the first year of nonrecognition, U.S. investment totaled 80 million (U.S. dollars), an all time annual record high. The ROC believes the superiority of its products will help it to survive competition from the PRC, even with the U.S. granting MFN to the PRC. (146)

The road to increased U.S.-People's Republic of China trade is still not yet smooth. Despite the adoption of MFN for China, obstacles still remain. One event illustrated these continuing problems. During 1979, the U.S. Treasury sought to remove one obstacle by negotiating the issue of frozen Chinese assets held by U.S. banks for the previous thirty years. On February 1, 1980, 80 million (U.S. dollars) worth of Chinese assets in U.S. banks were released. The Chinese Communist leadership met this result with a demand that interest be paid on the amount at five per cent for the previous thirty years or about 200 million (U.S. dollars) in interest. This demand for retroactive interest has raised additional problems. If the U.S. banks accede to the demands, these same banks may be hit with a series of lawsuits from Chinese residing in Taiwan who also claim the 80 million (U.S. dollars). In fact, when the U.S. froze the assets during the Korean War, some of the Chinese had fled to Taiwan by that time and some of the accounts have

Taiwan addresses. Another remaining question is the unspoken question of U.S. assets in China – mostly physical assets held by such corporations as Exxon, General Electric, and Citibank – totaling 196.9 million (U.S. dollars); China still owes the U.S. about 30 million (U.S. dollars) plus interest for old railroad loans. (147)

A recurring question is how active might the U.S. pursue a more formal alliance arrangement with China. During the same week in the first part of January of 1980 the U.S. revealed it would sell the Republic of China on Taiwan 280 million (U.S. dollars) worth of anti-aircraft missiles and other defensive weapons, U.S. Secretary of Defense Harold Brown, visiting in Peking, expressed a willingness to discuss expanding professional contacts and exchanges between the defense departments of the U.S. and China. (148) During that visit, the Defense Secretary indicated that China's military hardware was over a decade behind that of the U.S. and the U.S.S.R. (149) China, ever alert for political opportunity on the international scene, had even opened talks with the Soviets in Moscow in October of 1979 and had toned down some of its harsh anti-Soviet rhetoric on "revisionism" in order to concentrate on a critique of Soviet foreign policy; observers were unsure if this represented a legitimate thaw in the relations between Peking and Moscow or was merely a time-saving device while Peking gets its house in order and builds its strength. (150)

While the Soviet invasion of Afghanistan has pushed the Carter Administration to seek closer relations with China, this Soviet action has emphasized how Western technology can be used in a military way by a totalitarian power despite its previous denials to the contrary. When the Soviets entered Afghanistan, the troops entered in trucks built at the Kama River plant which had been aided by U.S. technology and financing. (151) The U.S. also allowed exports for the Soviet Union's Zil truck complex even though information had been obtained that the complex was producing not only military trucks but missile launchers. Lawrence J. Brady, former Deputy Director and Acting Director of the Office of Export Administration at the Department of Commerce, had testified that lax procedures have allowed the Soviets and other Eastern European nations to gain U.S. technology and knowhow which can be, and is being, used for military purposes. (152) Finally resigning from the Commerce Department in protest of the policies, Brady refuted the argument that if the U.S. did not supply the technology, then it could be obtained from U.S. allies: such technology of other nations is not that far advanced in certain fields as that of the U.S. and the "time lag" in technology which would result from the Soviets obtaining it from non-U.S. sources would be a legitimate objective of U.S. foreign policy. He cited the Kama River plant since if the U.S. did not participate, there may have been a five to six year delay in completing it. The Soviets continue to make a major effort to obtain information on new and emerging technology which may not have reached the military application phase in the U.S. but which has the potential for such use. (153) The same lax procedures and lack of control over technology for military use going to the Soviet Union may only be repeated in the case of the People's Republic of China. The U.S. and the Western powers may find in future years a strong China, once a willing friend, turned into a powerful and military adversary, through the acquisition of Western trade, financing, and technology. The Soviet Union in an editorial in *Pravda* at the end of January of 1980 lectured the U.S. that it should accept the fact of waning U.S. power and growing Soviet might and that present conditions enabled the Soviet Union to block U.S. moves and accomplish its own purposes in the world. (154) The same threat to the U.S. and Western and Asian nations of the Free World could come one day from the People's Republic of China. Warning that Communism uses the charade of detente only to gain additional strength with the help of Western financing and Western technology, Alexander Solzhenitsyn has stressed that Communism excels at such charades. His warning is one that the Free World may ignore only at its own peril:

> Communism is unregenerate; it will always present a mortal danger to mankind. It is like an infection in the world's organism: it may lie dormant, but it will inevitably attack with a crippling disease. There is no help to be found in the illusion that certain countries possess an immunity to communism: any country that is free today can be reduced to prostration and complete submission.
>
> In expectation of World War III the West again seeks cover, and finds Communist China as an ally! This is another betrayal, not only of Taiwan, but of the entire oppressed

Chinese people. Moreover, it is a mad, suicidal policy: having supplied billion-strong China with American arms, the West will defeat the U.S.S.R., but thereafter no force on earth will restrain communist China from world conquest. (155)

FOOTNOTES

(1) Franz H. Michael and George E. Taylor, *The Far East in the Modern World*, New York: Holt, Rinehart and Winston, Inc., 1964, p. 458.

(2) Claude A. Buss, *The People's Republic of China*, Princeton, New Jersey: D. VanNostrand Company, Inc. 1962, p. 50.

(3) *Ibid.*, pp. 50-51.

(4) Michael and Taylor, *The Far East*, pp. 460-461. Of course, the ideological campaign launched against businessmen was part of the general campaign to provide for ideological conformity and eliminate independent thinkers. Writers and artists were the victims of later campaigns. *Ibid.*, p. 462.

(5) Richard L. Walker, *China Under Communism: The First Five Years*, New Haven, Connecticut: Yale University Press, 1955, pp. 273-274.

(6) *Ibid.*, pp. 276, 280.

(7) Michael and Taylor, *The Far East*, pp. 466, 467.

(8) *Ibid.*, p. 473.

(9) Walker, *China Under Communism*, pp. 288-289.

(10) Michael and Taylor, *The Far East*, pp. 466, 467.

(11) *Ibid.*, pp. 494, 496, 499, 503-507.

(12) Derek Davies, "China: Rebirth of the Individual," *Far Eastern Economic Review*, August 17, 1979, pp. 51, 53.

(13) *Ibid.*, p. 53.

(14) "China: Economy," *Asia 1979 Yearbook*, Hong Kong: Far Eastern Economic Review Limited, 1978, pp. 172-173.

(15) Melinda Liu, "1979: One Step Backward for One Leap Forward," *Far Eastern Economic Review*, October 5, 1979, p. 78.

(16) *Ibid.*

(17) *Ibid.*

(18) Hua Kuo-feng, "Government Work Report" to the First Conference of the Fifth People's Congress on February 26, 1978, *People's Daily*, March 7, 1978.

(19) Cristine Russell, "China Trying to Leap Science Gap," *The Washington Star*, October 14, 1979, p. 1. Cristine Russell noted in an earlier article: "Assistance from the United States is considered crucial to achieving new modernization goals and an umbrella agreement in science

and technology was signed earlier this year when relations between the two countries were normalized." "China Bids to Master Advanced Sciences," *The Washington Star*, September 9, 1979. See "U.S.-China Science Agreements Signed," *Chemical & Engineering News*, 57 (February 5, 1979), p. 6.

(20) "Chinese Economists Discuss Planning National Economy," Peking, (Hsin Hua), November 22, 1979, "*Daily Report: People's Republic of China*, Foreign Broadcast Information Service, I (November 23, 1979), No. 227, p L9. This was a meeting of twenty economists and economic workers. It was a discussion jointly sponsored by the Economic Research Institute of the Chinese Academy of Sciences and the editing board of the journal *Economic Research*.

(21) "Jiefangjun Bao Article Comments on Anarchism," Peking, (Hsin Hua), November 23, 1979, *Daily Report: People's Republic of China*, Foreign Broadcast Information Service, 1 (November 29, 1979), No. 231, pp. 03-04.

(22) "Shanghai Economists Discuss Socialist Production," Peking (Hsin Hua), November 21, 1979, *Daily Report: People's Republic of China*, Foreign Broadcast Information Service, 1 (November 29, 1979), No. 231, pp. 03-04.

(23) "Economists Discuss U.S. Economic Situation," Peking (Hsin Hua) November 24, 1979, *Daily Report: People's Republic of China*, Foreign Broadcast Information Service, 1 (November 29, 1979), No. 231, p. B2.

(24) Shannon R. Brown, "Foreign Technology and Economic Growth," *Problems of Communism*, 26 (July-August, 1977), pp. 30-31.

(25) Antony C. Sutton, *National Suicide: Military Aid to the Soviet Union*, New Rochelle, New York: Arlington House, 1973, p. 16.

(26) *Technology and East-West Trade*, Office of Technology Assessment, Washington, D.C.: Government Printing Office, 1979, p. 206.

(27) *Ibid.*, pp. 206, 208.

(28) Sutton, *National Suicide*, p. 17.

(29) Miles M. Costick, *The Strategic Dimension of East-West Trade*, Washington, D.C.: American Council on World Freedom Task Force on Strategic Trade, 1978, p. 30.

(30) Alexander Wolynski, "Western Economic Aid to the USSR," *Conflict Studies*, (June, 1976), No. 72, p. 4. The author comments: "Normalization of Western trade and economic relations with Soviet Union and other Comecon countries would be desirable and welcome if circumstances were different; even the granting of economic aid would be feasible if this led to a true detente, proved by a diversion of domestic resources from military programmes to constructive economic development. But it would appear suicidal to subsidize the Soviet economy as long as it serves only to compensate for the drain on resources caused by military expenditure – in other words simply to sustain that military expansion, and, as some of its leaders believe, to diminish in the process Western resistance." *Ibid.*, p. 11.

(31) *Proposals for Reform of Export Controls for Advanced Technology, 1979*, Washington, D.C.: American Enterprise Institute for Public Policy Research, 1979, pp. 3-4.

(32) *Ibid.*, pp. 4-7. The question regarding a difference in attitude between the United States and its Western European allies on trade with the Soviet Union is discussed in Friedemann Muller, "East-West Trade and Security Policy," *Aussenpolitik*, 30 (1979), No. 2, 172-183. Western European nations look at the trade from a strictly economic viewpoint while the United States considers the economic and strategic importance of the trade.

(33) *Ibid.*, p. 6. It was noted that computers, aircraft engines, integrated circuitry and navigation systems are some of the items very similar in both military and civilian aircraft.

(34) Robert K. Dornan, "Exporting American Technology: A National Security Perspective," *The Journal of Social and Political Studies*, 2 (Fall, 1977), p. 140.

(35) R. Sean Randolph, "In U.S. Trade with Russia, Is our Security to be Sold," *Los Angeles Times*, August 15, 1979, p. 7.

(36) Statement by the AFL-CIO Executive Council on *Export Administration Act*, Chicago, Illinois, August 8, 1979, p. 1.

(37) *Proposals for Reform of Export Controls for Advanced Technology, 1979*, p. 6.

(38) Mark E. Miller, "The Role of Western Technology in Soviet Strategy," *Orbis*, 22 (Fall, 1978), p. 563. The author notes: "By Soviet criteria, this approach has worked rather well. The overall military technology gap between the United States and the USSR has narrowed appreciably in the past ten to fifteen years. A recent Defense Department survey of American and Soviet strength in thirty-two key weapon and command-and-control systems found the United States ahead in fifteen areas, the USSR ahead in twelve, and leadership in the remaining areas uncertain. More disquieting, however, is the very large and dynamic military R & D program, which, in the opinion of some experts may enable the USSR to achieve superiority in this critical area in the 1980's." *Ibid.*

(39) Charles M. Kupperman, "The Soviet World View," *Policy Review*, 7 (Winter, 1979), pp. 61-62.

(40) Wolynski, "Western Economic Aid to the USSR.", p. 11.

(41) "Technology Transfer and Export Controls," *National Security Record*, The Heritage Foundation, No. 13 (September, 1979).

(42) Seymour E. Goodman, "Soviet Computing and Technology Transfer: An Overview," *World Politics*, 31 (July, 1979), pp. 539, 568.

(43) *Proposals for Reform of Export Controls for Advanced Technology, 1979*, pp. 2, 3; Randolph, "In U.S. Trade with Russia, Is our Security to be Sold?, p. 7.

(44) Sutton, *National Suicide*, pp. 89-117. See also Antony Sutton, *Western Technology and Soviet Economic Development 1930 to 1945*, Stanford, California: Stanford University Press, 1977.

(45) Ibid., pp. 134-135; "Carter's Cover-Up at Kama River," *Human Events*, September 15, 1979, pp. 1, 8; "Commerce Aide Lifts Lid on Kama River Project," *Human Events*, December 8, 1979, pp. 1, 8. For a further discussion of the issues involved in the Kama River project and debate over export control legislation, see "Exporting Technology — Can Trade and National Security Coexist?" *National Journal*, August 18, 1979, pp. 1370-1374.

(46) "Carter's Cover-Up at Kama River," p. 1.

(47) Carl Gershman, "Selling Them the Rope: Business and the Soviets," *Commentary*, 67 (April, 1979), p. 36. The author provides a perceptive historical view of the period of great optimism for expanding Soviet trade and the continued resulting failure to do so.

(48) *Ibid.*, p. 45. A thorough discussion of the main elements of debate over technology is included in the "Commentary" by J. Fred Bucy, "Technology Transfer: We're Still Selling Them the Rope," *Government Executive* (September, 1978), pp. 37-41. One of the most recent examples of the controversy over exchange of technology involved a Control Data Corporation proposed computer equipment sale worth $2 million to the Soviet Union. Defense Secretary Harold Brown recommended against the license because it violated criteria established by the U.S. and a NATO committee which reviews arms and technology reports. Brown noted that there was a concern with national security since the computer could be applied in antisubmarine warfare. Len Ackland, "Computer Deal Tests U.S. 'Light Switch Diplomacy'", *Chicago Tribune*, October 22, 1979, Section 4, page 7.

(49) "Cultural Examinations Are Necessary," *People's Daily* (editorial) October 23, 1977.

(50) Talk by Chou Pei-yuan, Vice Chairman of the Chinese Communist Institution of Science, in Tokyo, United Press International dispatch from Tokyo, Japan, September 28, 1978.

(51) "Everybody Should Learn Technology," *People's Daily* (editorial), August 7, 1978.

(52) Seminar on "Employees' Spare Time Education," convened by National Federal of Unions, *Kuang Ming Daily*, August 14, 1979.

(53) "Anti-Chinese Report" by Suslov at the February meeting of the Soviet Communist Central, *People's Daily*, April 27, 1964; "July 14 Public Letter" from the Soviet Communists, *People's Daily*, July 20, 1963.

(54) "Boldly March On, Quicken the Pace," commentary by Hsin Hua correspondent, September 16, 1978.

(55) Hsin Hua dispatch from Peking, January 2, 1979.

(56) Central News Agency dispatches from Tokyo, February 28, 1979, and March 1, 1979. The Chinese Communists notified Japan on February 19, 1979 to suspend thirty-four contracts worth 2.8 billion (U.S. dollars) which had been signed after December 16, 1978. One of the contracts included was one for the New Japan Steel Corporation to help China build a steel company at Paoshan, Shanghai. News of the contract suspension shocked Japanese enterprises and sent prices downward on the Tokyo stock market.

(57) "Do Things According to Economic Rule, Speed Up Realization of Four Modernizations," by Hu Chiao-Mu, *People's Daily*, October 6, 1978.

(58) James Reardon-Anderson, "Science and Technology in Post-Mao China," *Contemporary China*, 2 (Winter, 1978), pp. 37, 39, 44. The author quotes the words of Chairman Hua Kuo-feng to the Fifth National People's Congress at the end of February, 1978: "For our economy to

develop at high speed, we must break free from conventions and use advanced techniques as much as possible." *Ibid.*, p. 37.

(59) M. D. Fletcher, "Industrial Relations in China: The New Line," *Pacific Affairs*, 52 (Spring, 1979), p. 94.

(60) "Concentrate All Energy on Production Construction," *People's Daily* (editorial), January 1, 1979.

(61) Hsin Hua dispatch from Peking, September 25, 1977.

(62) *People's Daily*, September 17, 1978.

(63) Kang Shih-en's speech at the production adjustment meeting for the Northeast district on August 30, 1979, Hsin Hua dispatch from Shengyang, September 4, 1979.

(64) See *People's Daily*, September 4, 1979; Hsin Hua dispatch from Canton, October 18, 1978; Hsin Hua dispatch from Peking, August 19, 1978.

(65) Central News Agency, special dispatch from Bonn, Germany, November 9, 1978.

(66) "To Boost the Productivity of Wool Textile," Hsin Hua correspondent report from Shanghai, July 19, 1979.

(67) *Ta Kung Pao* (Chinese Communist newspaper), Hong Kong, January 19, 1971.

(68) La Hsien-men's discussion with visitors from Japan, *World Commerce Weekly*, December 3, 1978.

(69) Shannon R. Brown, "Foreign Technology and Economic Growth," *Problems of Communism*, 26 (July-August, 1977), p. 40.

(70) Teng Hsiao-ping's statement in Tokyo on his return from his visit to the United States, AFP dispatch from Tokyo, February 7, 1979.

(71) "Why Can't the Blind Production of Ordinary Lathes Be Stopped?," Hsin Hua dispatch from Peking, December 14, 1978. See also *People's Daily*, June 28, 1979.

(72) "The Fixed Capital for Mines, Industries and Enterprises Should Not Be Used Without Compensation," Hsin Hua dispatch from Lanchow, March 24, 1979; "Why the Equipment That Cost 50 Million Yuan Has Been Sound Asleep for 16 Years," *People's Daily*, May 26, 1979; *Liberation Daily*, Shanghai, January 20, 1979.

(73) Chalmers Johnson, "The Failure of Socialism in China," paper presented at the Eighth Sino-American Conference on Mainland China, Institute of International Studies, University of South Carolina, Columbia, South Carolina, May 18, 1979 published in *The Enduring Chinese Dimension: Proceedings of the Eighth Sino-American Conference on Mainland China May 17-20, 1979*, Columbia, South Carolina: Institute of International Studies, University of South Carolina, 1979, pp. 29, 41.

(74) Paul Marer, "The Future for Trade With China," *Business Horizons* 22 (April, 1979), p. 6.

(75) Julian M. Sobin, "New Doors Into China: The Role of Technological and Commercial Exchanges," *Harvard Magazine*, (October, 1976), p. 55.

(76) Miriam London and Ivan D. London, "One Billion Chinese: The Phoney Market," *Barrons*, January 1, 1979, reprinted in *Conservative Digest*, (March 1979), p. 14.

(77) *"Doing Business With China"*, U.S. Department of Commerce, Industry and Trade Administration, Washington, D.C.: U.S. Government Printing Office, 1979, p. 1

(78) *Ibid.*

(79) President Carter's Remarks to Reporters, December 15, 1978, *U.S. Policy Toward China July 15, 1971-January 15, 1979*, Department of State, Selected Documents, Bureau of Public Affairs, Office of Public Communication, p. 47.

(80) Secretary Vance's Address at the Department of State Briefing on China, January 15, 1979, *U.S. Policy Toward China*, p. 57.

(81) Remarks by Juanita M. Kreps, Secretary of Commerce, Department of State Briefing on China, January 15, 1979, *Ibid.*, p. 58. She did mention that despite optimism, the U.S. needed to approach the trade question realistically: the trade would be highly competitive; other industrial countries using low interest credits had already won a significant share of the China market; limitations remained on China's hard currency earning capacity; U.S. exports to China cannot be financed by Eximbank credits and Chinese exports to the U.S. do not receive most favored nation (MFN) tariff treatment. (Note: Both houses of Congress voted MFN treatment for China on Thursday, January 24, 1980).

(82) Remarks by W. Michael Blumenthal, Secretary of the Treasury, at the Department of State Briefing on China, January 15, 1979, *Ibid.*, pp. 59-60.

(83) "U.S. China Sign Trade Accord," *The Washington Star*, July 8, 1979, p. A7; Hobard Rowen, "U.S. Signs Pact to Grant China Favored Status," *The Washington Post*, July 8, 1979, pp. A1, A9; Bob Livernash, "China Trade Agreement," *Congressional Quarterly*, October 27, 1979, p. 2423; Vladimir N. Pregelj, "Most Favored Nation Policy Toward Communist Countries," Library of Congress, Congressional Research Service, Major Issues Systems, March 28, 1979; Susan Woodard, "MFN Trade Status and the P.R.C.," *Issue Bulletin*, The Heritage Foundation, No. 55, November 19, 1979; George D. Holliday and John P. Hardt, "China-U.S. Trade," The Library of Congress, Congressional Research Service, Major Issues System, April 3, 1979.

(84) U.S. policy that has a direct trade with China (as well as the Soviets and Eastern Bloc nations) includes the following three categories: export licensing controls that govern the export of products or technologies appearing on a list of controlled commodities, and nuclear equipment and nuclear fuels; controls over export and import facilities that regulate the use of credits, loan guarantees, or other incentives for trade with certain categories of nations; and control over tariffs that allows the United States to levy higher rates of duties on imports from countries to whom "most favored nation" (MFN) status has not been granted. *Technology and East-West Trade*, Office of Technology Assessment, Washington, D.C.: U.S. Government Printing Office, 1979, p. 111. A view of the major considerations in granting "most favored nation" status to China and key issues is contained in Susan Woodard's "MFN Trade Status

and the P.R.C.," *Issue Bulletin*, The Heritage Foundation, No. 55, November 19, 1979.

(85) "The Red China Myth," *The China Post* (July 6, 1979), p. 2.

(86) *Ibid.*

(87) "China Economic Research Monthly," Japan Trade Promotion Association, June, 1979; Central News Agency, special dispatch from Bonn, Germany, August 8, 1979; AFP dispatch from Tokyo, August 16, 1979.

(88) "Peiping's Suspension of Purchase Contracts," *The China Post*, March 12, 1979. It noted that some of the Japanese firms had already geared production schedules to the contracts when they were notified by Peking. The firms involved including Nippon Steel, Hitachi, Toshiba, and Komatsu lost ground on the Tokyo stock market. The editorial noted that Peking's exchange reserves are estimated at 2.1 billion (U.S. dollars), an insufficient amount to finance its ambitious purchases from abroad. It cited two additional factors: China needed to use part of its foreign exchange to import food grain to feed its increasing population and the continuing power struggle within the Chinese hierarchy with Teng Hsiao-ping pushing modernization while Hua Kuo-feng and others have criticized the program for being too costly and unrealistic. The newspaper editorial did point out a long range significance to the event: "We may say that the suspension of contracts with Japanese firms is not an isolated affairs (sic), it reflects many problems that should not be lightly ignored . . . Peiping's faithlessness serves as a warning to U.S. and European companies which hope to do trade with Red China."

(89) William R. Kintner and John F. Copper, *A Matter of Two Chinas: The China-Taiwan Issue in U.S. Foreign Policy*, Philadelphia, Pennsylvania: Foreign Policy Research Institute, 1979, pp. 30-31.

(90) *Ibid.*

(91) *Ibid.*, p. 34.

(92) Susan Woodard, "China: The Mythical Market," *Backgrounder*, The Heritage Foundation, No. 77, March 7, 1979, p. 22.

(93) *Technology and East-West Trade*, p. 283.

(94) Kintner and Copper, *A Matter of Two Chinas*, pp. 33-34.

(95) Norma Schroder, "Economic Costs and Benefits," in Ramon H. Myers, Editor, *Two Chinese States: U.S. Foreign Policy and Interests*, Stanford, California: Stanford University Press, 1978, p. 27.

(96) Premier Sun Yun-suan's Address at the Dinner of the American Chamber of Commerce in the Republic of China (January 16, 1979), *Free China Weekly*, January 21, 1979, p. 2.

(97) Susan Woodard, "China: The Mythical Market," *Backgrounder*, p. 3.

(98) "Western Executives Expect Record Sales at China Fair," *Chicago Tribune*, (October 29, 1979), Section 4, page 8.

(99) Norma Schroeder, "Economic Costs and Benefits," in Ramon H. Myers, Editor, *Two Chinese States: U.S. Foreign Policy and Interests*, pp. 30-33. Louis Kraar has written: "There is no way, however, to avoid the weeks of discussions required to do business in China today. Nor is

there any survival manual that prepares U.S. executives for the many practical difficulties of operating in an environment that requires exceptional self-reliance. It can be quite a chore merely to communicate with your home office." He notes that American executives may have to punch out their own telex tapes at the Peking Telegraph Building, have difficulty finding lodging, pay outrageous prices for mediocre meals and for Chinese-made goods which are available in the United States. Louis Kraar, "China: Trying the Market Way," *Fortune* (December 31, 1979), p. 54.

(100) Joseph Winski, "'China Trade' Means Wealth, But It Won't Come Easily," *Chicago Tribune*, (September 20, 1979), section 4, pp.1, 12. Kenneth Lieberthal, a consultant for the State Department on China and presently associate professor of political science at Swarthmore College, observed: "But in trying to gauge the outlook for investment in the People's Republic, it always pays to recall the political and ideological context in which decisions about such matters are made in that country. The context today seems basically favorable to trade and investment. However, it is not hard to imagine some contingencies in which real setbacks would be possible." Kenneth Lieberthal, "China: The Politics Behind the New Economics," *Fortune* (December 31, 1979), p. 44.

(101) Jim Stepanek, "A Ten-Year Profile on The Bank of China." *The China Business Review* (September-October, 1979), pp. 10-11. An observer of the China scene has noted: "Good coordination among the various ministries and local government bodies on these issues has often been lacking in the past, as was exemplified most painfully by the expansion of the Wuhan Iron and Steel Complex by German interests. To run at full capacity, the finished unit requires more electricity than is produced in the entire province." Lieberthal, "China", *Fortune*, p. 47.

(102) Nicholas Ludlow, "A Guide to Barter in the China Trade," *The China Business Review* (September-October, 1979), pp. 10-11.

(103) Frank Ching, "McDonnell Nears Pact With China on Sale of Jets," *The Wall Street Journal*, (October 11, 1979), p. 6.

(104) *Recognizing the People's Republic of China: The Experience of Japan, Australia, France, and West Germany*, Report prepared for the Subcommittee on Asian and Pacific Affairs of the Committee on Foreign Affairs, U.S. House of Representatives, 96th Congress, 1st Session (May, 1979), p. 4.

(105) Shih Ming-shong, "The Prospects for Trade and Modernization in Mainland China," Eighth Sino-American Conference on Mainland China, Institute of International Studies, University of South Carolina, Columbia, South Carolina, May 18, 1979, *The Enduring Chinese Dimension*, p. 86. Professor Shih of National Taiwan University divides the performance of China's foreign trade over the past three decades into three subperiods: the steady expansion of the 1950's, the slowdown and leveling off of the 1960's, and the accelerated growth of the 1970's. He notes: "Now let us assess the ability of Communist China to mobilize its domestic capital and the factors which determine her import capacity. During the 1979-1985 periods, mainland China needs $600 billion in capital, if inflation is not taken into consideration. That is to say mainland China must accumulate

roughly US$86 billion per annum or 27 per cent of its GNP. In a low income nation like Communist China, it is hard to maintain a high investment ratio for more than one quarter of GNP; especially in a society with an increasing degree of openness and liberalization the demonstration effect can not long be suffocated. Hua, Teng and other Chinese Communist leaders remain committed to the vision of an economically self-sufficient country, and the purchases they have sanctioned are more than anything else an attempt to safeguard the nation's economic future. Every plant or piece of equipment which is purchased now, it is hoped will in the long run reduce the need to buy manufactured goods from foreign countries." *Ibid.*, pp. 77, 83.

(106) Keng Piao's conversation with the Director of the Broadcasting Bureau of the Japan Broadcasting Association, dispatch of *Japan Times*, Peking, August 13, 1979.

(107) Cristine Russell, "China Trying to Leap Science Gap," *The Washington Star*, October 14, 1979, p. A9.

(108) Kentaro Koshiba, "Red China Business Unpredictable," *Japan Times*, reprinted in *The China Post*, March 12, 1979.

(109) Edward N. Luttwak, "Seeing China Plain," *Commentary* (December, 1976), p. 32.

(110) "Big Trade With China? A Japanese Dream Ends," reprinted in *Chicago Tribune*, August 10, 1979, section 1, p. 8.

(111) Pai Wong-hsiang, Director of the Department of Mainland Affairs of the Kuomintang Central Committee, "Communist China Using External Economic Links to Pursue Worlwide Political Schemes," *Free China Weekly*, September 16, 1979, p. 2.

(112) See Robert Sutter, *Playing the China Card: Implications for United States-Soviet-Chinese Relations*, Report Prepared for the Subcommittee on Asian and Pacific Affairs of the Committee on Foreign Affairs, U.S. House of Representatives, 96th Congress, 1st session (October, 1979), and "China-U.S.-Soviet Relations: Should We Play the 'China Card'?", Library of Congress, Congressional Research Service, Major Issues Systems (November 13, 1979).

(113) Fox Butterfield, "China Showing Interest in Buying U.S. Warplanes," *The New York Times*, (March 8, 1979), p. A5; Richard Burt, "Study Urges U.S. Aid to Chinese Military," *The New York Times*, October 4, 1979, pp. A1, A8.

(114) Brian Crozier, "The China Mirage," *National Review*, (December 7, 1979), p. 1544. See Franz Michael, "Moscow and Peking: Past, Present and Future of Sino-Soviet Relations," pp. 250-265, in John Tierney Jr. (Editor), *About Face: The China Decision and Its Consequences*, New Rochelle, New York: Arlington House, 1979.

(115) Luttwak, "Seeing China Plain," *Commentary*, p. 33.

(116) "Easing the Way for China Deals," *Far Eastern Economic Review*, November 23, 1979, p. 66.

(117) Fox Butterfield, "Leading Peking Dissident Loses Appeal in High Court," *The New York Times*, (November 8, 1979), p. A3; Fox Butterfield, "China Dissident Likens Present to the Repressive Past," *The New York Times*, (November 15, 1979), p. A22; "Excerpts from Peking Trial Transcript," *The New York Times*, (November 15, 1979), p. A22; Jay

Mathews, "Peking Sentences Dissident to 15 Years," *The Washington Post*, (October 17, 1979), pp. A1, A28. See also David Finkelstein, "Repression in China: A Few Speak Out," *The Washington Post* (October 28, 1979).

(118) Statement of Amy Young-Anwaty, regarding Most Favored Nation Trading Status for the People's Republic of China, before Subcommittee on Trade, Committee on Ways and Means, U.S. House of Representatives, November 29, 1979, pp. 1-3.

(119) *Some Recent Developments Related to Human Rights in the People's Republic of China*, Committee on Foreign Relations, United States Senate, 96th Congress, 1st session (March, 1979), pp. 16-17. Although the report saw some real and immediate gains for human rights in this post-Mao period, the evidence given hardly made the case: "While the number of political prisoners confined in prisons and labor camps in the PRC is not known, it *appears* scores of thousands of people have been released and *unknown numbers* of others have had their damaging labels as rightists removed." (Italics mine). *Ibid*, p. 17. A thorough study of the background of human rights in Maoist China can be found in Warren Kuo's "Oppression and Persecution in Communist China," pp. 305-328, in *Case Studies on Human Rights and Fundamental Freedoms: A World Survey*, The Hague, Netherlands: The Foundation for the Studies of Plural Societies, 1975. See also the authoritative early report: Richard L. Walker, *The Human Cost of Communism in China*, prepared at the request of the Subcommittee to Investigate the Administration of the Internal Security Laws, Committee on the Judiciary, U.S. Senate, 1971, reprinted by the ACU Education and Research Institute, January, 1977.

(120) "China (the People's Republic of)," *Amnesty International Report 1978*, London: Amnesty International Publications, 1978, pp. 154, 156-158. In the 1979 report, Amnesty International denounced a "dangerous" rise in political arrests in China especially activists who are calling for more democracy and that long-term imprisonment without trial and execution of dissenters was occuring in China, "Amnesty Group Details Global Pattern of Abuse," *The Washington Star* (December 10, 1979), p. A8.

(121) Report of the American Institute in Taiwan, "AIT Report," *The China Post*, (November 13, 1979), p. 2; Robert G. Sutter, "Taiwan's Future: Implications for the United States," The Library of Congress, Congressional Research Service, Major Issues System, October 22, 1979, p. 4; William R. Kintner and John F. Copper, *A Matter of Two Chinas: The China-Taiwan Issue in U.S. Foreign Policy*, pp. 25-26, 37; Donald J. Senese, "Challenge of the Future: The Advancement of the Newly Industrializing Countries," *The Journal of Social and Political Studies*, 4 (Fall, 1979), No. 3, pp. 248-250.

(122) Sutter, "Taiwan's Future," pp. 4, 6. The report to the Subcommittee on Asian and Pacific Affairs by the Foreign Affairs and National Defense Division of the Congressional Research Service of the Library of Congress noted that private and commercial transactions will form "the bedrock" of U.S. relations with Taiwan. It noted that trade is a good indicator of relations. In the last year of official United States-Taiwan

relations, two-way trade reached eight billion (U.S. dollars); two-way trade in the first year of "derecognition" will reach about ten billion (U.S. dollars). The report noted that despite derecognition (and recognition of Peking) by Japan, Australia, West Germany and France, Taiwan's economic relations with each of these nations increased in the year following derecognition except for exports to France which had been on a steady decline before this action. *Recognizing the People's Republic of China*, pp. vii, ix.

(123) See Donald J. Senese, "Reassessments for Taiwan, Japan and South Korea: U.S. Reliability in Asia" in Tierney (ed.), *About Face*, pp. 356-378.

(124) David Nelson Rowe, *U.S. China Policy Today*, Washington, D.C.: University Professors for Academic Order, 1979, pp. 16-18. Mainland China has acted to turn its opposition to even sympathetic supporters. While France recognized Communist China in 1964, four years later, during China's Cultural Revolution, the Chinese Communist press and Chinese Communist diplomats in France encouraged leftist demonstrations to bring down the government of the man who had led the way to this recognition, Charles DeGaulle. *Recognizing the People's Republic of China*, p. 4. Harold Wilson, former Prime Minister of Great Britain, was one of the leading advocates of recognizing and dealing with the PRC. While on a tour of the U.S. in the fall of 1979, Harold Wilson expressed his disillusionment with the PRC and noted that the Red Chinese are "untrustworthy." See "Voice of Experience," *The China Post* (October 6, 1979), p. 2.

(125) Susan Woodard, "China: The Mythical Market," *Backgrounder*, p. 23. The *China News* (March 17) pointed out that negotiations were going on between the U.S. and Communist China on textiles observing: "The U.S. market for textiles is finite. So what the Chinese Communists are able to sell to the Americans will hurt the textile exporters of Taiwan, Japan, South Korea, and Hong Kong. When it comes to the price of the cheapest goods, the Chinese Communists will be able to compete effectively. Their wages sell at a loss temporarily, if that is competitively advantageous," "No bonanza," reprinted in *Free China Weekly*, (May 20, 1979), p. 3.

(126) Julian Weiss, "Taiwan Bounces Back," *Asia Mail*, September, 1979, pp. 1,14.

(127) Pai Wong-hsiang, "Communist China Using External Economic Links to Pursue Worldwide Political Schemes," *Free China Weekly*, (September 16, 1979), p. 2.

(128) "The China Trade I: First Contacts," *World Traffic*, September 24, 1979, p. 37.

(129) Jay Mathews, "Chinese Seek Grasp of Western Laws," *The Washington Post*, (November 25, 1979), p. A28.

(130) "Peking's People Exports," *Far Eastern Economic Review*, (November 30, 1979), pp. 68-69.

(131) "National College Entrance Test for People's Republic of China," *HEW News*, U.S. Department of Health, Education and Welfare, November 26, 1979; Spencer Rich, "China's College Bound Youths Trail America's in

Science," *The Washington Post*, (November 29, 1979), p. A13.

(132) "Hua's Window-Shopping Tour," *Far Eastern Economic Review*, (November 16, 1979), p. 16.

(133) Derek Davies, "China: Rebirth of the Individual," *Far Eastern Economic Review*, p. 51.

(134) U.S. Representative Richard T. Schulze, *Congressional Record*, January 24, 1980, H202. Eight members of the House Ways and Means Committee – Representatives Ed Jenkins, John J. Duncan, Bill Archer, Phil Crane, Jim Martin, L.A. Bafalis, Richard T. Schulze, and John H. Rousselot – filed a dissenting view on the MFN legislation. They urged five steps which should be taken before MFN be granted to China: 1) the President should send a supplemental message to Congress clarifying whether certain assurances had been obtained from the PRC; 2) the Chinese government should pay the $50 million it owed the Export-Import Bank; 3) the Chinese government should negotiate some type of financial settlement to cover the $220 million it owes in outstanding bond notes; 4) the U.S. should negotiate a bilateral textile agreement to ease the potential job losses for Americans in labor intensive industries; and 5) the Carter Administration should send an internationally recognized organization like Amnesty International to the PRC to investigate alleged human rights violations. "Supplemental Views on House Concurrent Resolution 204," *Approving the Extension of Nondiscriminatory Treatment to the Products of the People's Republic of China*, House Ways and Means Committee, House Report No. 96-733, pp. 12-13.

(135) *Ibid.; Congressional Record*, January 29, 1980, E211. A thorough discussion of how MFN would affect U.S. nonrubber footwear and other leather product industries can be viewed from the testimony of F.A. Meister, president of the American Footwear Industries Association. See Senator Barry M. Goldwater, "The Unanswered Questions of MFN for Communist China," *Congressional Record*, S445-S448.

(136) *Ibid*, H215.

(137) *Ibid.*, H207.

(138) *Ibid.*, H214.

(139 *Ibid.*, H217.

(140) "Most-Favored-Nation Status of People's Republic of China," *Congressional Record*, January 28, 1980, E137-E138.

(141) *Congressional Record*, January 24, 1980, H220, S351.

(142) "MFN. Status to Peiping," *The China Post*, January 28, 1980, p. 2. See R. C. Longworth, "Soviet Invasion gives China Big Boost in Trade with U.S." *Chicago Tribune*. February 21, 1980, Section 4, p. 9.

(143) Ku Cheng-kang, "Better New Relationships for Greater Common Interest," Speech delivered July 17, 1979, S-2.

(144) "China's Asian Neighbors Feel Stirring of Economic Giant," *The Korea Herald*, December 19, 1979, p. 4; "Asia Feels Stirring of China Economy," *Chicago Tribune*, January 5, 1980, Section 4, p. 7.

(145) "BOFT dissects U.S.-Red 'most-favored-nation"; no threat," *The China Post*, January 26, 1980, p. 1.

(146) "Record Year for Foreign Investment,"; *Free China Weekly*, January 13, 1980, p. 4; "Melody Lingers On," *The China Post*, January

16, 1980, p. 2; "U.S.-ROC Relationships," *The China Post*, January 19, 1980, p. 2; "ROC's Trading Partners," *The China Post*, January 21, 1980, p. 2; "U.S. Investments in Taiwan," *The China Post, January 28, 1980*, p. 2; "ROC's Economy Steadier," *The China Post*, January 29, 1980, p. 1; Barry Kramer, "Taiwan Still Thrives A Year After the Loss of U.S. Recognition," *The Wall Street Journal*, February 8, 1980, pp. 1, 31.

(147) "A Peking Puzzle for the Americans," *Far Eastern Economic Review*, February 15, 1980, pp. 56-57. See "China (PRC) – Update: MFN for the People's Republic," *Asia Report*, The Center for Strategic and International Studies, Georgetown University, Volume I, No. 3 (February, 1980), pp. 1-3.

(148) "This Week" *Far Eastern Economic Review*, January 18, 1980, p. 5. See Robert Crabbe, "Chinese Seek U.S. Alliance To Quell Soviet Aggression," *The Korea Herald*, January 10, 1980, p. 4.

(149) "Peiping Is A Paper Tiger," *The China Post*, January 12, 1980, p. 2.

(150) David Bonavia, "First Stop on the Way to the Gulf," *Far Eastern Economic Review*, January 11, 1980, p. 13.

(151) "The Kama River Source," *The Wall Street Journal*, February 8, 1980, p. 14. The editorial noted that it was time to cut away secrecy from technology transfers: "It is more likely the files would show even more serious lapses than the one involving Kama River. Intelligence sources believe that the Soviets could not have installed multiple warheads on their intercontinental missiles as quickly as they have if a U.S. firm had not been permitted to sell them a unique machine that produces high quality miniature ball bearings. Congressional sources, backed by independent intelligence estimates, claim that U.S. technology helped the Russians develop guidance systems and gyroscopes for ICBMs and anti-submarine devices that make U.S. Trident submarines more vulnerable." Columnist Jack Anderson writes less subtlely: "Any suggestion that American officials and businessmen helped the Soviet Union invade Afghanistan would raise cries of outrage from the White House and Wall Street alike. Unfortunately, it happens to be true." See Jack Anderson, "Technology of U.S. Benefits Soviets," *The Washington Post*, February 6, 1980, and "Soviets Deftly Raid the U.S. Store," *The Washington Post*, February 18, 1980. Also Rep. Ron Paul, "Transfer of U.S. Technology Benefits Soviets," *Congressional Record*, February 13, 1980, E566-E567.

(152) Lawrence J. Brady, "Statement of Lawrence J. Brady before the Subcommittee on Investigations of the Committee on Government Affairs," U.S. Senate, February 20, 1980. He warned in his testimony: "The United States should begin to take the military impact of computers more seriously. It should continue to seek technological advancements to maintain its qualitative edge over potential adversaries, but export controls are a necessary adjunct to effective research in maintaining this edge. Only controls can help to frustrate the actual application of U.S. technological sophistication to use in the Soviet military . . . Essentially, we do not know even how many computers have been exported to the Soviet Union, nor what most of them are being used for." *Ibid.*, pp. 17, 19.

(153) *Ibid.*, p. 27. See Raymond Coffey, "Carter Assailed for Techno-

logical Aid to Soviets," *Chicago Tribune*, January 24, 1980, Section 1, p. 7.

(154) Henry S. Bradsher, "Pravda Editorial Lectures U.S. on Diminished World Role," *The Washington Star*, January 31, 1980.

(155) "Another Warning for the West from Solzhenitsyn," *The Washington Star*, February 17, 1980, p. G-4.